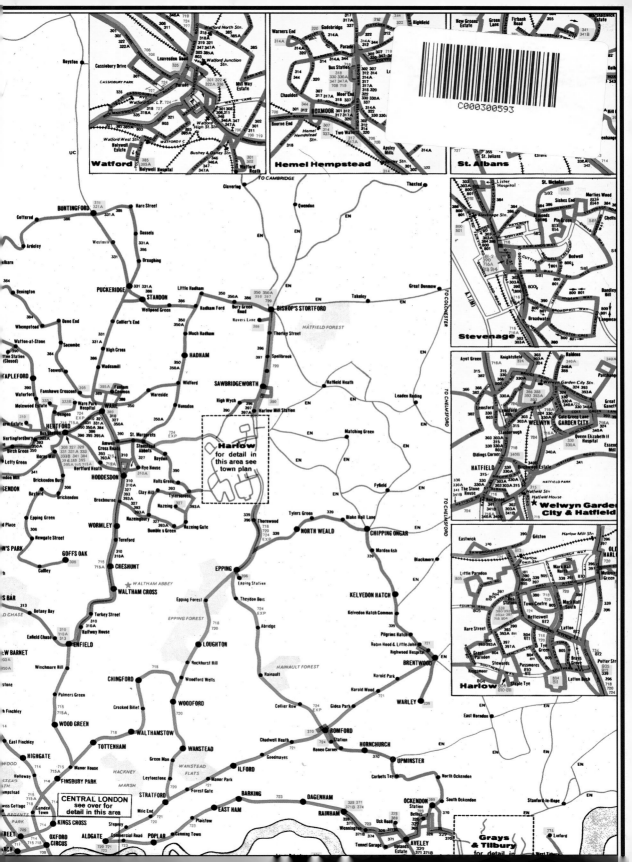

LONDON
COUNTRY

LONDON
COUNTRY

John Glover

Ian Allan
PUBLISHING

Front cover: Chilternlink-branded Leyland National SNB514 at High Wycombe. *Barry Le Jeune*

Back cover, top: Following pioneering by Surrey of Ramblers' Bus, other leisure services were introduced in Kent and Herts. This is the 318 Lea Valley Leisure Bus (or Lee Valley, according to which sign you read). It is operated here by Leyland National SNB163, now demoted from its coach status. It can be seen in its former guise on page 118. *Trevor Whelan*

Back cover, bottom: Routemaster coach RMC1517 on Green Line duty in Stevenage. *Barry Le Jeune*

Endpapers: London Country Bus & Green Line coach map, 1973.

Title page: The Leyland National was the standard bus for the National Bus Company subsidiaries, and London Country had a fleet of 543. This is SNB (Short National Bus) 383, a series B version, moving to the righthand lane in Kingston Road, Ewell, on a 478 Kingston-Bookham Station working in February 1987. It is about to turn right down Ruxley Lane. The Leyland Olympian on the 406 behind it will continue straight ahead at this point. *John Glover*

Half Title page, top to bottom: Long-standing route 406 ran from Kingston (Greater London) to Redhill (Surrey). Leyland Atlantean AN193 is passing Surrey's County Hall on a summer afternoon in 1981. *John Glover*

The radiator grille of a Routemaster is unmistakable, especially in the Green Line version with the twin headlights. This is RMC1469, new to Hertford in August 1962, one of a fleet of 66 coaches. *John Glover*

The London Country fleetname in full NBC style on one of the few RTs to receive the leaf-green livery applied during the latter days of NBC ownership of the company. *John Glover*

First published 2006

ISBN (10) 0 7110 3121 5
ISBN (13) 978 0 7110 3121 0

© Ian Allan Publishing Ltd 2006

Published by Ian Allan Publishing

an imprint of Ian Allan Publishing Ltd, Hersham, Surrey KT12 4RG.
Printed in England by Ian Allan Printing Ltd, Hersham, Surrey KT12 4RG.

Code: 0611/B

Visit the Ian Allan Publishing website at
www.ianallanpublishing.com

Contents

Dedication

This book is dedicated to the memory of Donald Allison MBE, FCIT who, as Public Transport Co-ordinator for Surrey County Council 1974-89, richly deserved his award which was made for services to public transport.

Introduction

The story of this company, which was a far from typical bus operation, deserves to be recounted. An outline of some of the main elements of its history appears below. The full extent to which records survive has not been explored, but some at least remains in the files of the County Councils and others.

London Country Bus Services Ltd (LCBS) was the former Country Area of London Transport Buses, itself created as part of the LPTB Act of 1933. The Country Area had a somewhat turbulent history, covering as it did anything from new towns like Stevenage, Crawley, Harlow and Hemel Hempstead to the more rural parts of Essex and Surrey, where it came up against the small independent operator. The company also operated Green Line coaches, where a day's work for a driver (and originally a conductor) was to drive from a garage on one side of London to the other and back again.

The rising tide of car ownership in the postwar era, particularly prevalent in the Home Counties, did nothing for bus patronage. At the same time it made bus operation ever more difficult and unreliable.

Separation from London Transport took place on 1 January 1970 and the company became part of the National Bus Company. Shorn of London Transport's protection, LCBS became very dependent on external subsidy. This was provided by the main counties in which the company operated, Hertfordshire, Surrey, Kent, Essex, Buckinghamshire, Berkshire and West Sussex. But this did not take effect until the 1974-75 financial year, when the County Councils took on the new responsibilities enshrined in the Local Government Act 1972.

Thus began an uneasy relationship in which the County Councils were expected to meet rising deficit bills of a commercial organisation, but at the same time the licensing arrangements with the Traffic Commissioners remained unchanged. The County Councils had little in the way of powers, but were left with heavy responsibilities. Meanwhile, the company had to provide a bus service in what was subsequently recognised to be a deteriorating financial situation.

The fleet problems in the mid-1970s were sufficiently severe that not only were some Reliances with three-plus-two seating acquired from Barton Transport, but they were deemed 'suitable' for Green Line use. This is Eccleston Bridge, Victoria, with a 714 arriving from Dorking in April 1976.
Barry Le Jeune

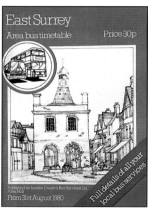

The relations with the former London Transport parent became difficult at an early stage, exemplified by the shortage of spare parts for buses in the mid-1970s. LT gave its own operations priority, but this left LCBS in a very difficult position, as at that stage a large proportion of its fleet was of LT design and the effect on its ability to run the services was disastrous.

The County Councils pursued various initiatives. In Surrey, the aim was to get operating costs down, and a major plank of this was the replacement of London Transport services which still penetrated the county by the lower-cost LCBS operation. In effect, green buses replaced red ones over substantial areas of the county. That did not mean like-for-like replacement; for a start, the services were to operate out of different garages, and the portion within what was then the Greater London Council (GLC) had to be examined carefully, since any subsidy required needed to be paid by someone. More generally, all services were examined critically for what they achieved, and some former LCBS services were moved to independent operation.

Fares reached very high levels everywhere, and disputes arose as to whether fares should vary according to route profitability or should be uniform throughout the operation. Concessionary fares for the elderly were expanded.

Above left: The traditional LT bus stop flag, in this case the version with a compulsory stop for buses and a request stop for coaches. The plates are for 406 (Kingston-Redhill), 408 (West Croydon-Guildford), 468 (Epsom-Chessington Zoo), 470 (West Croydon-Dorking), 703 (Baker Street-Dorking) and 727 Express (Crawley-Heathrow-Luton Airport). *John Glover*

Left: During the period when London Country timetables covered all bus services in their respective areas, this is the East Surrey book with a well-known Reigate landmark on the cover, dated 31 August 1980. *Author's collection*

Below: In the 50th year of Green Line in 1980, this special addition to the normal livery was made on DV1, one of just two Volvo B58s tried experimentally, seen here at Golders Green in May 1981. *Barry Le Jeune*

There were positive traffic developments in expanding areas, and Stevenage Superbus was one such initiative promoted by Hertfordshire.

Declining reliability of Green Line due to traffic congestion presented its own problems. Attempts to combine Green Line operations with local buses foundered for this reason. Latterly, Green Line operations terminated in central London, at Victoria, or Oxford Circus, rather than continuing on a cross-London basis, though the Aldgate services had always terminated there. This avoided exporting the problems, so to speak, but the writing was on the wall for the central London services and they ceased progressively.

One of the company's major investments took place at Tinsley Green, Crawley, where a new bus servicing facility was built. On the other hand, several garages were closed to save overheads. New buses were decidedly utilitarian; whether this was the right approach in well-moneyed areas may be questioned, but the financial imperatives were acute.

This state of affairs continued until the Transport Act 1985 brought about deregulation of bus services outside London and at the same time the National Bus Company was wound up and its constituent companies privatised. LCBS was broken into four operational companies (London Country North West, North East, South East and South West) and each was sold separately during the late 1980s.

That was the end of LCBS as such, but there was a major problem following the way in which the companies were sold, although this was little recognised at the time. The garages were to be sold separately and then leased back to the bus companies for a 10-year period. In an area of high land values, garages were later sold for redevelopment and the bus companies were left without premises from which to operate. As they were never more than marginally profitable, this caused huge upsets in service provision, the echoes of which continue today.

The author was a public transport co-ordinator for Surrey County Council between 1974 and 1989.

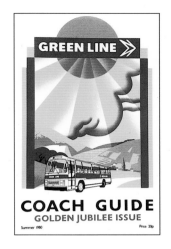

Top: The cover of the 1980 Golden Jubilee issue of the Coach Guide design was an update of that which appeared on the first-ever Green Line guide for 1930, half a century earlier.
Author's collection

Above: There were 10 Area books, each with a local picture theme on the cover. This is Knole House, National Trust, on the Sevenoaks book, dated 24 September 1983.
Author's collection

Left: The National Bus Company double arrow logo with the company name, as applied to a Leyland National bus.
John Glover

1 Development of the Country Bus

'It was not long before the motor bus disturbed the tranquility of London's countryside.'

J. S. Wagstaff

EARLY DAYS IN LONDON

London's first regular horsebus service was started by George Shillibeer (1797-1866) on 4 July 1829, the same year that the Stephensons' *Rocket* locomotive established its place in the history books at the Rainhill trials. It ran from the suburb of Paddington via Regent's Park to Bank in the City and the five-mile journey usually took an hour.

New services sprang up, with rival bus operators competing for passengers, often racing each other to pick up fares. By the 1840s the horsebus had replaced most of the short stagecoach operations. This was too much for Shillibeer, who went bankrupt. But where he failed, others succeeded.

In 1855, the London General Omnibus Company (LGOC) was established and became the largest omnibus operator in London. It was originally an Anglo-French enterprise, the Compagnie Generale des Omnibus de Londres. It bought out hundreds of independently owned buses and established a consistent level of service for its fleet. Within a year the LGOC controlled 600 of London's 810 omnibuses. Other large operators later included the London Road Car Company and Thomas Tilling & Co.

Operating a horsebus was an expensive business, given the number of horses needed, the costs of stabling, feed and vets' fees, as well as the cost of the bus itself. It was not until 1904 that the first mechanically driven bus appeared. Growth of motorbuses meant that the last horsebus ran in London in 1914. After that, the need in its mechanical replacement was for greater reliability and development generally. Thus solid tyres were replaced by pneumatics and the petrol engine by diesel. Vehicles grew in length to carry more, and the open top was enclosed. The seating area on the upper deck was upholstered and extended above the driving position. New suspension systems avoided the 'boneshaker' epithet, and a windscreen was fitted to give some protection for the driver.

The vehicles were licensed as fit to operate by the Metropolitan Police, who adopted their own ideas of what was, or was not, acceptable. A further development was the relaxation on the maximum vehicle width to (a still narrow) 7ft 0in, thus making it possible to provide a gangway for the conductor between rows of forward facing seats.

By the beginning of the 20th century, the other public transport service providers in London were the horse and later electric trams, the main line railways and the underground railways.

THE COUNTRY AREA

But while all this was going on in London, in what became the Country Area bus services were also being developed. Twenty or so miles south of central London, the East Surrey Traction Company started motorbus operations between Reigate and Redhill on 23 May 1911. This was only the first stage, but expansion brought the company to the attention of the General. This company had already extended some of its services into the Country Area, both to provide recreational weekend services to give Londoners days out, and also as an early attempt to provide services between the small towns in the vicinity and London.

LGOC also had its own ideas as to how the largely undeveloped area south of the capital would be served when it was built up. But even if the concept of territories holds good, cross-boundary services are still needed to bridge the 'no man's land' in between.

The upshot was the concoction of a working arrangement in which the A25 (Valley) road running east-west between Sevenoaks and Guildford constituted the boundary. East Surrey could use this road and run anywhere to the south, but would also be permitted to penetrate northwards to Merstham, Kingswood, Caterham and Westerham Hill, and to run anywhere in Reigate borough.

This collaborative agreement persisted, with modifications. Thus in 1921, new terms resulted in the LGOC providing 'all the motor omnibuses required' together with 'all the garages sheds and equipment required to keep the services operated on behalf of the LGOC within the London country area'. East Surrey paid the LGOC a proportion of the fares income on a monthly basis, and leased the garages.

Dunton Green was the first garage to be opened under this arrangement in 1922. It was strategically placed to serve the area between Tonbridge, Sevenoaks and Bromley, and the premises accommodated 12 vehicles on opening. It was followed by Chelsham, Godstone, Leatherhead and Swanley, all in 1925. Reigate remained wholly owned by East Surrey.

NATIONAL

The same sort of thing happened to the north of London. Here, the LGOC itself established a garage in Watford and by agreement took over services operated by the London & North Western Railway as feeders to its rail services in 1920. The operation of three LGOC routes was transferred from Cricklewood to Watford, and those crews were paid at the 'London rate'. The other services were seen as Country routes, and paid at a lesser rate. This provoked strike action and the Country routes and premises were passed to the National Omnibus & Transport Company the following year, 1921. This was the origin in the differential pay rates between Central and Country buses, which then became a fixture in such negotiations. It also had unanticipated consequences in future years, then still far away.

National started operations in central London in 1909, but by agreement with 'The General' moved out to concentrate on operations in a wider area which in some cases extended well beyond any London-related boundaries. Here too there were other independent operators, such as Hertford & District Motor Services. This latter was essentially a local company, and thus in 1921 received the licences, then administered by Hertford Council, for routes to Braughing and Bishop's Stortford, in preference to National. By 1924,

The first London General Omnibus Company mechanical vehicle licensed for service was this Clarkson steam bus of 1904. It was a beginning, and its legacy to the street cleaners was less noxious than the horsebus. *Author's collection*

however, its considerable network had sold out to National, which also took over the Hertford & District's premises in Ware.

In 1921, however, National too concluded an agreement with the LGOC in the same manner as East Surrey, though with lesser freedom of action on areas in which they could operate other than 'for and on account of General'.

Similar events took place elsewhere in the area as a whole. Notably, the Thames Valley company had, from 1922, a looser arrangement with General to run services west of the capital. In the south-west, a 1927 agreement between LGOC, Aldershot & District and East Surrey determined who could run on which roads and in 1928 East Surrey took control of Autocar Services of Tunbridge Wells.

THE LONDON TRAFFIC ACT 1924

The London Traffic Act 1924 established the London & Home Counties Traffic Advisory Committee, whose area, bounded by St Albans, Gravesend, Dorking and Slough, closely matched that which a decade later became the Special Area of the London Passenger Transport Board when it was set up in 1933.

One of the effects of the Act was that the control and regulation of bus services in the Metropolitan Police District, itself then extending beyond the present Greater London area, became the responsibility of the Police themselves. A principal concern was the regulation of the number of buses permitted to ply on certain streets, to relieve traffic congestion (sounds familiar!) and to protect tram services from competition. The Metropolitan Police Public Carriage Office, as licensing authority, was established to approve bus routes, the bus crews themselves, the suitability of the vehicles and service frequencies. Fares, however, were not their concern.

This AEC K-type double-decker, No29, was built for the East Surrey Traction Co Ltd of Bell Street, Reigate, carrying the name of Arthur Henry Hawkins, whose enterprise resulted in a bus service between Reigate and Redhill. This completely open-top double-decker lacked any protection from the elements for the driver. He did, however, have the benefit of a horn to warn other road users. It entered service on 27 July 1920 and was bodied by Brush, whose body number, 4953, is visible under the canopy. It lasted just under 10 years in service. *Ian Allan Library*

Outside the Metropolitan Police area, it may be said here, this was a matter for local authorities, not all of whom had relevant powers. Even those that had powers, derived from the Town Police Clauses Acts of 1847 and 1889, exercised them very variably, if at all. Nevertheless, would-be operators had to obtain licences in any location where they were issued.

The Metropolitan Police Chief Constable, A. E. Bassom, had the responsibility of devising a route-numbering system which avoided duplication of numbers across this area by the different operators, and put some order into the result. Consequently, the Bassom numbering system, as it became known, provided for the following:

1-299	London General Omnibus Company
300-399	National and London General Country Services
400-499	East Surrey and London General Country Services
500-599	Thames Valley operations west of London, and others.

Another feature of the Bassom system was the use of suffix letters to denote short workings, though in practice this soon also covered minor deviations from the basic route and other variations. The principle of a main route number in each case was however retained.

ROUTE DEVELOPMENTS

While many of the bus services instituted in the early years in the Country Area were very local in nature, some longer-distance links between London and the outskirts were established. Thus, although the Charing Cross, Euston & Hampstead Railway (a forerunner of the Northern Line) only reached the then-isolated outpost of Golders Green in 1907, a daily bus service thence to St Albans (84) was established in 1913. This followed the formation of the Underground Electric Railways of London group (UERL), which included the LGOC, as well as all the underground lines then in existence except the Metropolitan.

That same year also saw a Hounslow-Windsor service (81) and Bromley-Westerham Hill (95). These and others supplemented the various summer Sunday-only services which were already running. Such activity came to an end for the duration of World War 1, but was reinstated afterwards. Many routes then in existence became established, and some survive in a recognisable form today. Vehicles to provide the services also developed to become cheaper and more effective as time progressed.

RAILWAY BUSES

Another source of competition was the main line railways. The Great Western Railway had been very early in the field of running its own buses as feeders to its rail operations, and the same approach was used with varying degrees of enthusiasm (and success) by other railway companies.

Just as the growth of the electric tramcar made inroads into urban steam railway carryings in the early years of the 20th century, counteracted in the south of London by railway electrification, the spread of bus competition encouraged the railways to develop their own services.

However, the legal basis of road operations by railway companies was at best shaky, and in 1927 each of the 'Big Four' railways together with the Metropolitan Railway deposited Bills in Parliament aimed at regularising the situation. The LGOC was amongst those bodies objecting, and one result was that the Metropolitan's Bill was declared 'not proved' and proceeded no further. The Metropolitan's only excursion into bus operation was that between its decidedly remote Watford terminus and the centre of Watford.

The other Bills giving the general powers needed were, however, passed as the Railways (Road Transport) Act 1928, though services which both picked up and set down in the Metropolitan Police District were excluded, and tramways were protected from such competition. What was to become the London Transport monopoly area of bus operation drew ever closer, though railway incursion into bus operation looked set to become more serious, and this was one of the reasons for the setting up of London General Country Services.

Above: A mere seven years after the mechanical bus put in an appearance, the last horsebuses ran in 1911. This is the scene at London Bridge on 25 October that year. It only preceded the demise of the electric tramcar in London, at least for the time being, by 40 years. *Author's collection*

Above right: It was not long before London General expanded its services to the Country Area, as this picture of a K-type (apparently) on an 85 to Putney Bridge suggests. In those days, the countryside reached a good bit nearer central London. *Author's collection*

ROAD TRAFFIC ACT 1930

One of the landmark Acts of Parliament for transport was the Road Traffic Act 1930, which contained the basis of public service vehicle licensing and operation. There were two main elements.

First, there were the vehicles and their drivers — the quality requirements. Henceforth, each vehicle had to have a certificate of fitness for purpose and to be inspected annually. Then, the operator needed to obtain a public service vehicle (PSV) licence in respect of each vehicle, and to show that he was a fit and proper person to hold such a licence. In addition, drivers and conductors each had to obtain a licence, the issue of which was based on character as well as technical competence. Though the Act has been updated more than once, this is still broadly the situation today.

Quantity licensing was also introduced by the 1930 Act, which was another matter altogether. The holding of a Road Service Licence (RSL) became a necessity before an operator could run a local service, known in those days as a stage-carriage service. This stated the route and stopping places, the timetable, the operator, the fares to be charged and any other conditions that the issuing body, the area Traffic Commissioner, was minded to require.

Applications for RSLs and changes to existing ones were published in a fortnightly journal, Notices & Proceedings, and objections could be lodged by other operators and interested parties such as local authorities. The formal grounds specified in the Act on which the Commissioners made their decisions were:

- suitability of the route
- the adequacy of existing services on that route
- the desirability of the new service in the public interest, and
- the general needs of the area.

Some principles emerged over time, concerning both the protection of existing operators, and how 'public need' might be construed.

The first was that of protection. Generally, existing operators holding RSLs were given protection from the competitive or predatory incursion of others. The aim was that they should with confidence be able to offer a complete service on the route at all times, without risking the loss of some of their revenues. In its day, this would have been seen as 'wasteful competition'.

The other was public need. This came to be interpreted as encouraging cross-subsidisation between routes as well as within them. Thus, given that the operator held a number of RSLs for profitable and effectively protected services in the area, that same operator could be expected to run some unprofitable services where a public need might be demonstrated. In effect, he would provide a public service at his own expense.

Thus the situation emerged of bus companies with something approaching monopoly rights in the areas they served, offering comprehensive services throughout the operating day and at weekends, at fares which were not unreasonable. The whole was overseen indirectly through a public body. There was clearly a balance to be struck, sometimes a very delicate one in terms of the 'additions' which a company could reasonably be expected to shoulder, or where new services operated by another were complementary to the existing ones rather than predatory. Even so, major problems were relatively few in the years in which the system operated.

It might be added that none of the detailed means of determination was ever set out formally, but that was the effective position — and it worked. Or, more accurately, it worked for as long as the bus industry generally was profitable. If profitability were to decline, the ability to support poorly performing parts of the network would also decline. That situation, however, was still a long way away, and was of little relevance in the area under discussion. Not, that is, until the establishment of London Country Bus Services Ltd as a subsidiary of the National Bus Company in 1970.

LONDON GENERAL COUNTRY SERVICES

As will have become clear, the relationship between The General and East Surrey was close, and this culminated in the former acquiring the latter in 1929. This paved the way for further acquisitions and amalgamations, but it was also a defence mechanism to deter the railways.

The railways in general, and the Southern Railway in particular, had been finding it more satisfactory to buy into bus companies which could then be influenced to operate feeder services to and from their stations, rather than undertaking the direct provision themselves. Thus were born companies such as Southern National and Western National, incorporating parts of the National undertaking as their core, and Southern Vectis. It also accounts for how part of the bus industry became publicly owned under the Transport Act 1947.

By 1932, what had become London General Country Services Ltd was fully established as the major bus operator in the country parts of the London Transport area as would shortly be specified, although at this stage there were a number of small independents still in existence. London General Country Services had already formed Green Line Coaches Ltd in 1930 as a wholly owned subsidiary to provide longer-distance services of a coaching nature. This was essentially a competitive move to outsmart other operators, in which it was largely successful.

Not all the service reorganisations undertaken in this period were successful. Thus it was intended to exchange service provision in the Banstead area of Surrey between the LGOC and LGCS. The 80/180 routes from Morden to Lower Kingswood/Walton-on-the-Hill would have become operated by LGCS in 1932, had it not been for union opposition. The *status quo* then remained for half a century, the transfer finally taking place under rather difference circumstances on 24 April 1982.

LONDON TRANSPORT, 1933

While the quality provisions of the 1930 Act had universal applicability — and, as amended, still do — the quantity provisions did not apply to London as such, at least until the formation of London Country in 1970 and then only to operations outside the Greater London Council area.

With the setting up of the London Passenger Transport Board, a number of geographical areas were created as part of the London Passenger Transport Act of 1933. Much of this was to give statutory effect to the agreements which had already been developed in the last couple of decades or so.

Autocar's main area of operation was in Kent. The company was later acquired by East Surrey, and this early AEC Regent shows how the roofing-in of the upper deck was achieved, albeit still with an open staircase at the rear. Like the East Surrey K-type, it shows Arthur Henry Hawkins on the side along with a legal address of Bell Street, Reigate, though in fact it was at this stage an AEC demonstrator which went to Autocar in August 1929 and was later taken into East Surrey stock as No255. Bodywork was by Shorts of Rochester and at the time it was the only closed-top double-decker in the fleet. *AEC/Ian Allan Library*

The areas (see Map on page 16) were:

- **The Board's Special Area**

  The outer boundaries included Welwyn, Harlow, Brentwood, Gravesend, Sevenoaks, Reigate, Guildford and Slough. This was basically the area established under the 1924 Act, but more tightly drawn in places, notably the north-east and the west. A Road Service Licence from the Traffic Commissioner was not required, but the Board were permitted to operate only on routes approved by him. Within the Special Area, no other body could operate local bus services without the written consent of the Board.

- **The London Passenger Transport Area**

  This extended the boundaries in the north to Tring, Luton, Hitchin and Bishop's Stortford, and in the south to East Grinstead, Crawley and Horsham. Outside the 'Special Area' but within the London Passenger Transport Area, the Board were able to operate stage or express carriage services, but for this purpose required the grant of a Road Service Licence from the Traffic Commissioner under the terms of the Road Traffic Act 1930. The London Traffic Area boundary was conterminous with the Special Area to the north and south of London, but extended further west in places, and also further east, notably so to destinations such as Pitsea and Billericay.

- **Beyond the London Passenger Transport Area**

  The Board had very limited powers to operate to certain specified destinations such as Ascot, Aylesbury, Royston and Tunbridge Wells. Conversely, other operators from outside the Area were allowed to run to destinations within the Area, to enable them to reach sensible terminating points.

These definitions gave the Board something approaching monopoly powers for its road services over a huge area. Thus in 1933 the entire London Passenger Transport Area served a population of 9.4million in a territory which covered 1,986sq miles. Of that, 1,550sq miles were in the Special Area, as defined.

In effect, this map and the associated provisions were to determine the operating territory of Country Buses for the next 37 years and, in practice, for a good deal longer still.

2 The London Transport years

(In 1947), 'almost everyone was blind to the prospect of a large increase in the number of private motor cars and the problems that that would produce'.

T. C. Barker & R. M. Robbins, 1974

As shown in the last chapter, the newly formed London Passenger Transport Board (LPTB) was given wide powers to operate bus services, more or less as it chose and to the exclusion of others. The new territory was determined with reference to the existing operating areas of provincial groups. Hitchin to Crawley is roundly 60 miles, while Slough to Grays/Gravesend is about 40 miles. This created a number of border towns, such as Harlow, Tonbridge, Guildford and High Wycombe.

What, however, were the objectives of the 1933 LPTB Act? There were four principal requirements:

- That the Board should operate a self-supporting, unsubsidised, system
- That unification of provision should take place under public control
- That its management would be by a non-political body
- That the main line railways would participate, but without transfer of ownership.

It may be noted that the Board was not a nationalised undertaking; in the event, that was to come rather later, in 1948.

A NEW IMAGE

Action took place on many fronts, including fleet renewal and new uniforms, while bus shelters appeared selectively. Bus stop signs were erected, initially at all the important boarding and alighting points, and many

London Transport Country Bus Routemaster RML2423 is seen on the long-defunct route 306 to Leavesden. This is High Barnet in September 1969. The RMLs had an extra bay inserted in the body as can be seen here with the central small window; Country operations didn't have any 'ordinary' RMs. *John Glover*

SCALE OF MILES
0   5   10

ROYSTON

BALDOCK
LETCHWORTH
BUNTINGFORD
HITCHIN   COTTERED
BRAUGHING

DUNSTABLE
BISHOPS STORTFORD
IVINGHOE
LUTON
WELWYN
AYLESBURY
HARPENDEN   HERTFORD
TRING   HARLOW
WENDOVER   HEMEL HEMPSTEAD   HATFIELD
ST. ALBANS
GREAT MISSENDEN   CHESHAM   CHESHUNT   CHIPPING ONGAR   INGATESTONE
LITTLE MISSENDEN   POTTERS BAR   EPPING
WEST WYCOMBE   RADLETT   SHENFIELD
AMERSHAM   WATFORD   BILLERICAY
HIGH WYCOMBE   RICKMANSWORTH   BUSHEY   BARNET   ENFIELD   LOUGHTON   BRENTWOOD   WICKFORD
LOUDWATER   BEACONSFIELD   NORTHWOOD   WARLEY   PITSEA
R. Thames   HENDON   TOTTENHAM   ROMFORD
FARNHAM ROYAL   HARROW   ILFORD   NORTH OCKENDON
UXBRIDGE   BARKING
SLOUGH   EALING   R. Thames   RAINHAM
MAIDENHEAD   HOUNSLOW   GRAYS
WINDSOR   ERITH   TILBURY
STAINES   RICHMOND   DARTFORD   GRAVESEND
VIRGINIA WATER   EGHAM   WIMBLEDON   MEOPHAM
ASCOT   CHERTSEY   KINGSTON   BROMLEY   CHISLEHURST
SUNNINGDALE   ESHER   CROYDON   ORPINGTON
OTTERSHAW   WEYBRIDGE   FARNBOROUGH
EPSOM   OTFORD   WROTHAM
WOKING   KEMSING
BROOKWOOD   OLD WOKING   LEATHERHEAD   CATERHAM   SEVENOAKS
REDHILL   GODSTONE
DORKING
GUILDFORD   REIGATE
SHERE   EDENBRIDGE   TONBRIDGE
GODALMING   HORLEY   LINGFIELD
EWHURST   POUND HILL   EAST GRINSTEAD   TUNBRIDGE WELLS
CRAWLEY   FOREST ROW
TURNERS HILL
HORSHAM

REFERENCE

 Board's " Special Area."
Board's Area outside " Special Area."
Boundary of London Passenger Transport Area.
Boundary of London Traffic Area (1924).
Boundary of Metropolitan Police District.
Boundary of Administrative County of London.
Unrestricted Outward Runnings by the Board.
Restricted Outward Runnings by the Board.
Inward Runnings by Outside Proprietors.

NOTE :—Within the " Special Area " no person other than the Board may, except with the written consent of the Board, operate stage or express carriages carrying passengers local to that Area except in certain minor cases specified in Section 16 of the London Passenger Transport Act, 1933. Outside the " Special Area " and within the London Passenger Transport Area the Board may operate stage or express carriages subject to the provisions of the Road Traffic Act, 1930, and to the grant thereunder of road service licences from the Traffic Commissioners. Included within the London Passenger Transport Area at 30th June, 1934, there were 183 Administrative Areas as follows :—The City of London, The City of Westminster, 9 Counties, 3 County Boroughs, 27 Metropolitan Boroughs, 34 Municipal Boroughs, 78 Urban Districts and 30 Rural Districts. The Area comprises 1,986 square miles with a population estimated at over 9,400,000.

of these carried timetable cases. From 1935 bus stops began to be provided universally in the Central Buses area. This later spread to Country Buses, but complete coverage was never achieved. Local timetable booklets were produced. New bus stations were built at Dorking, Hertford, Sevenoaks and Windsor, while a new livery consisting of mid-green bodywork with apple green window frames, black lining, a silver roof and orange wheels became universal.

All this was provided by what was set up as the LPTB's Country Bus & Coach Department. There were economies of scale to be had too, for items which were common to all bus operations. Centrally provided services included engineering, accountancy, publicity and uniforms and from 1935 the overhaul of at least the more modern vehicles was transferred from Reigate to Chiswick Works. Again, this doubtless seemed a sensible idea at the time, but it also meant that Country Buses, still being put together from a multitude of operators, would never have the attributes and resources of a free-standing bus company.

Also established were Green Line Coaches, which were worked from Country Bus garages, but by separate crews. This demarcation reflected different pay scales from those of ordinary bus work, though there were numerous examples of interworking.

To identify the routes to the public, the LPTB built further on the Bassom numbering system. The revised arrangements were:

1-299	Central Buses
300-399	Country Buses, north
400-499	Country Buses, south
500-699	Trolleybuses
letter codes	Green Line coaches

This system endured until a little beyond the period covered by this book, except that Green Line coaches were numbered in the 700-799 series in the postwar years. The only variations of note in the Country Bus area were the selective adoption of local route-numbering systems such as the C routes in Crawley and SB (for Superbus) in Stevenage. Accommodation had also to be made in cases of joint operations with other companies, though such instances were relatively few.

A separate problem was the exhaustion of route numbers, and limited use was made of the 800-series by London Country. In the Central Area, the 500-series numbers made surplus by the demise of the trolleybuses were used for the new Red Arrow services distributing passengers from London rail termini.

In more recent times, the various successors to London Country have often reverted to simpler single or two-digit numbers, and some of the resulting vacancies have been purloined by London Buses for its own use on completely unrelated routes. Many of the 3xx and 4xx series numbers however survive, for buses plying similar routes to those of the 1950s or even as far back as the 1920s.

DIVIDED TOWNS

The acquisition of private bus companies continued, or in some cases separations of such companies or disposals, to match the fleet and service provision more precisely with the London Passenger Transport Area as defined in the 1933 Act. Service reorganisation was meant to provide a more rational and less overlapping service pattern, though this was to cause problems at the edges of the areas.

Boundaries are an inherent problem for public transport, the whole aim of which is to bring people together and link them to places to which they otherwise would have no access.

The concept of a ring of towns 30 miles or so from central London, to which the Country operation might extend, was in many ways sound. These were the natural boundaries of services radiating from the centre and

Left: The AEC lowbridge buses were designed for an important purpose, despite the limited vertical dimensions that would result. This is RLH32 in Guildford on a 436 in the early days of London Country in June 1970; London Country fleetnames have replaced London Transport on the sides. *Barry Le Jeune*

Below: The Guy Specials saw London Country service, just. This is a line-up of preserved vehicles at Dorking in 2005; real life did not require duplicates to operate to Coldharbour! *John Glover*

where they might meet the services of the territorial operators surrounding the capital. Thus in Guildford, Surrey, the services of London Transport's Country Buses would abut those of the Aldershot & District Traction Company. That London Transport also had statutory rights only backed up such a position.

The existence of a border town through which an operating boundary effectively passed meant that cross-town services were entirely lacking. However well-meaning the idea might have been, such a result was hardly likely to be in the best interests of the citizens of Guildford as a whole. Similar fates befell many other towns, including, for instance, Slough and Grays.

There was a secondary effect. The companies serving some of the larger towns also felt it necessary to maintain their own garages, and sometimes bus stations. In Guildford, the situation was further complicated by the opening this gave for independent companies to become established. Latterly, additional town services were operated by both Safeguard and Blue Saloon, while Tillingbourne operated on one of the radials from a rural base remote from the town centre. The situation thus saw the overhead costs of two main operators, but a complete lack of co-operation between them in service provision.

Situations varied from place to place. Dartford garage was originally built and owned by Maidstone &

District, but was taken over by the Board on 1 July 1933, along with Northfleet. The latter was formerly tram sheds, replaced by a new garage built by London Transport in 1937. It was only the second to be provided with full canteen facilities.

Overall, the industry was probably using rather more infrastructure than was really needed, although this was less important while service provision was profitable. It was however backed up by pay rates which were likely to be higher for Country Buses than the other operators, which led to entrenched positions in respect of any changes which might be contemplated.

STABILISATION

In their second Annual Report, for the year to 30 June 1935, the Board declared as follows:

'The transfer to, or the acquisition by the Board of the undertakings operating road services in the Board's Area has enabled the traffic requirements of that area to be reviewed as a whole. Out of a mass of unrelated and often conflicting services in the country areas, the Board have attempted to build a co-ordinated and regular system. In doing so, they have sought to preserve every necessary public facility and to anticipate to some extent the future requirements of the travelling public. The problem was troublesome in the country areas which had to be treated sector by sector until a complete programme had been built up… During the two years (from 1933), the principal consolidation schemes have related to the Dartford, Gravesend, Grays, Hemel Hempstead, St Albans and Watford districts, with further schemes for Amersham, Windsor and others at an advanced stage. Co-ordination schemes for the coach services were also being introduced.'

It is of interest also to note the then size of Country Bus & Coach, in terms of staff, when compared with the other activities of the LPTB:

LPTB staff by main group, as at 30 June 1935

	No	%
Railways	14,373	18.5
Central Buses	35,835	46.2
Country Buses and Coaches	5,563	7.2
Trams and Trolleybuses	19,747	25.5
Common Services	1,982	2.6
Total	77,500	100.0

Source: LPTB Annual Report 1934/35

The Country Bus & Coach department was thus a relatively small player in the total scene, and was never going to be in a position to influence greatly the direction taken by the undertaking as a whole. The railways, ie the Underground, are also noticeable for their relatively modest staff requirements, but in those days a complete train with its huge carrying capacity, like the buses, needed only two staff.

Unfortunately, the Board was reluctant to separate out most of the results below the level of 'buses and coaches', so there is little information on the Country Area as such.

WORLD WAR 2

Following the outbreak of war, an exodus of both population and business from central London took place. Large numbers of people settled in the Country Area and, in addition, war factories and military installations grew up. A drastic reduction in private motoring and petrol rationing contributed to a great expansion of Country Bus traffic.

During the course of the war, Country Bus mileage increased by 32%, while the traffic carried nearly doubled. The growth continued postwar, and in 1947, the last pre-nationalisation year, the mileage operated on Country Bus services was 92% higher than in 1933. The number of passengers was nearly three times as great. The population in the Country Bus area rose by roundly 35%.

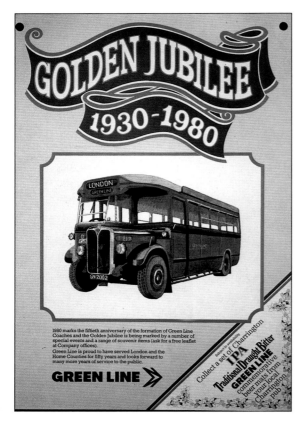

1980 marks the fiftieth anniversary of the formation of Green Line Coaches and the Golden Jubilee is being marked by a number of special events and a range of souvenir items (ask for a free leaflet at Company offices).
Green Line is proud to have served London and the Home Counties for fifty years and looks forward to many more years of service to the public.

GREEN LINE ⟩⟩

Green Line was established in 1930 and this colourful poster was displayed on Green Line stops in the 50th anniversary year of 1980. *John Glover*

Green Line coaches had a difficult war. Withdrawn in total on 1 September 1939 for conversion to ambulances, some were restored a few months later to ease acute transport problems, and by the end of 1940 all were again in service. Shortages of fuel saw them withdrawn again in 1942, this time for the duration.

THE 1950S FLEET

A major problem after the war was the age of the vehicles, themselves suffering from the lack of maintenance other than that which was unavoidable, and the influx of 'utility' vehicles in order to 'make do'. The saviour was to be the RT bus.

'The improved RT bus will undoubtedly mark a big step forward in the comfort of bus travel' enthused the 1944/45 Annual Report — but only, as it turned out, when sufficient resources could be obtained to enable the fleet to be built.

The use of 'pay-as-you-board' was in the postwar plans, but not as later adopted. Passengers boarded the bus and, as it progressed along the road bought their tickets from a conductor, who sat behind a desk. They then proceeded to a seat. Experiments on these lines proved unsatisfactory; labour shortages were to become serious, but bus operation by one staff member only, on any scale, was still years away.

The RT AEC Regent bus originally appeared just before World War 2, but quantity building was not possible until 1948-54. This 56-seater, of which the design varied little during construction, was allocated both to Country Buses and Central Buses. Similarly, the RLH lowbridge bus of the same era, with the sunken gangway on the upper deck to reduce the overall height significantly, was also allocated to both operating parts of London Transport.

The RF was in many respects the single-decker equivalent, produced between 1951 and 1952. The AEC Regal was built in both bus and Green Line versions, all those allocated to Country Bus & Coach having doors from the outset. Like the RTs before them, these were stalwart vehicles, and both were to give many years — perhaps *too* many years — of continuous service.

Then there were the GS buses, or Guy Specials. These were built for London Transport in 1953/54 by Guy Motors of Wolverhampton using the Guy Vixen lorry chassis as a basis, and featured a Perkins P6 engine. The 26-seat bodies were built by Eastern Coach Works of Lowestoft. London Transport took 84 of these for use on services in the Country Area. The radiator emblem was a Red Indian head, with the Guy Motors' motto 'Feathers in Our Cap' on the headband.

These four vehicle types were to form the backbone of the operations of the Country Bus & Coach department for the 1950s and, with the subsequent addition of the Routemasters, the 1960s.

THE MARKET

The 1920s and 1930s had seen a gradual outward movement of London's population as the following table shows, though allowances need to be made for the disruption caused by the war for the 1947 totals.

The outlook seemed bright for Country Bus & Coach. With a substantially increased population in their catchment area and the 'Green Belt' legislation heralding the construction of a series of New Towns, what more could they want?

London Passenger Transport Area
estimated population (thousands)

	County of London	Rest of built-up area	Total, built-up area	Outer Country zone	Total LPT area
Mid-1921	4,524	2,728	7,252	1,058	8,310
Mid-1933	4,299	3,538	7,837	1,521	9,358
Mid-1939	4,013	3,989	8,002	1,886	9,888
End-1947	3,305	4,040	7,345	2,175	9,520

Source: Annual Report LPTB 1946 and 1947, BTC 1948

The postwar period thus looked promising for Country Buses and Green Line; whereas the London, and particularly central London, population was set to decline, this was more than compensated for by the growth in what was then termed the 'Outer Country Area'. Rather larger than that which was later to become the Greater London area under the Greater London Council, that for Country Buses extended to Amersham, Luton, Harlow, Sevenoaks, Horsham, Woking and Windsor. The trend of outward population movements was to continue through the remaining period of London Transport stewardship.

The early results of what on 1 January 1948 became the nationalised London Transport Executive under the Transport Act, 1947 were quite encouraging:

Vehicle miles operated by LPTB/LTE (thousands)

	Central buses plus trams and trolleybuses	Country buses	Coaches	Total
1933/34	313,526	22,919	26,447	362,892
1938/39	343,288	28,586	27,604	399,478
1947	339,949	44,059	21,833	405,841
1956	319,160	47,208	24,171	390,539

Source: Annual Reports LPTB 1947, LTE 1956

The number of passenger journeys also grew satisfactorily, with both Country Buses and Coaches carrying well above the levels they had been accommodating before the outbreak of hostilities.

The 14-strong RC-class Green Line coaches were introduced by London Transport in 1965 and carried a unique grey livery with a green band. Here, RC11 is seen in the Hyde Park area. It is on a Windsor-bound service 705, and the board above the windows reads 705 SEVENOAKS WESTERHAM BROMLEY LONDON VICTORIA LONDON AIRPORT WINDSOR. 705. Notable is the reference to London Airport rather than Heathrow; Heathrow gained this title when Croydon was no longer London's airport, though presumably Gatwick was still considered insignificant at this stage.
AEC/Ian Allan Library

Green Line as it existed from the 1950s, until at least the coming of the Routemaster coaches. This is Golders Green on 9 April 1969 with a St Albans RF displaying full side boards on a 712 to Dorking, albeit as modified in the 1960s. *John Glover*

By the mid-1950s, the New Towns in the South East containing homes for much of the London overspill population were coming on stream. These were part of the 23 New Towns established in England and Wales after World War 2 under the New Towns Act 1946. Most were to the north of London:

- in Essex: Harlow
- in Hertfordshire: Hatfield, Hemel Hempstead, Stevenage and Welwyn Garden City
- in West Sussex: Crawley

Target populations for each, with the initial development completed, were between 23,000 (Hatfield) and 75,000 (Harlow), with both Hemel and Stevenage at 60,000. All were within the London Passenger Transport Area, as designated, and hence within the 'Country' remit. As with the wartime evacuees who were moved out of London to suburban towns during the bombing, the New Town settlers liked their surroundings, but they still needed that link with London. Green Line was in many ways the ideal means of transport.

Given also the decline in Central Area passenger journeys, the relative importance of the Country Bus & Coach operation was increasing, as the table shows. However, the passenger journey figures for 1955 were to be the highest that Country Bus & Coach was ever to record.

Passenger journeys (millions)

	Central buses, trams and trolleybuses	Country buses	Coaches	Total
1938/39	3,149	136	24	3,309
1947	3,399	266	25	3,690
1955	3,088	297	35	3,420

Source: Annual Reports LPTB 1947, LTE 1956

The chief development of note in the early 1950s was a revamp of the local services in the Grays and Tilbury area of Essex, formerly operated by Eastern National. On the formation of the London Passenger Transport Board in 1933, Grays had effectively been cut in half. Until then, local services had been operated by Eastern National, but from 1934 those in the west of the town centre fell to London Transport, leaving Eastern National with the services to the east. That was the end of cross-town services since, apart from anything else, Country Buses had no operating base in Grays. This was put right by the subsequent construction of a Grays (GY) garage, but operations remained divided.

The whole was transferred to London Transport on 30 September 1951 through an order made by the British Transport Commission. Services were rationalised to combine them with existing London Transport routes, with new through services which obviated the need to change buses, while others were converted to double-deckers. The Eastern National garage at Grays was closed and operations concentrated on the London Transport garage.

Country Buses also acquired the associated staff, vehicles and garage. Services were recast the following year, to re-create broadly the 1933 situation, albeit under different ownership.

Situations can be righted, but the inherent problems should not be underestimated. One of these has been the terms and conditions enjoyed by staff, which were usually more generous in London Transport and its successors than in the territorial bus companies. Thus a shift to an LT operation held the likelihood of increased operating costs from staff demanding (and probably getting) better rates of pay, while a shift in the other direction to a cheaper operation would also foster discontent for the opposite reason. In the postwar years anyway, labour relations were often distinctly fragile.

CHAMBERS

The Chambers Committee of Inquiry into London Transport was appointed by the Minister for Transport in 1953. The objective was to see what practical measures could be taken to secure greater efficiency and/or

One of the Daimler Fleetlines, XF7, allocated to East Grinstead garage, working to Reigate station on the 424. Originally, these buses had the upper deck closed off by a door when working in one-man mode. *Author's collection*

economy in the undertaking. It took place at what turned out to be around the high point of postwar travel volumes by London Transport, for many years to come.

The focus was, as usual, on the 'London' aspects, with Country Bus & Coach receiving little more than passing mention. It did, however, provide an insight into the financial position of those activities, which for the most part were carefully hidden in the Annual Report under the umbrella heading of 'Buses and Coaches'. Trolleybuses have been included as they were, in effect, a variant on Central Buses. The last trams ran in 1952, the previous year.

Thus the situation in 1953 was as shown in Table 1.

Table 1: London Transport Road Operations 1953
by section of business

	Central Buses	Trolleybuses	Country Buses	Coaches	All road operations
Number of passenger vehicles	6,543	1,716	1,068	372	9,699
Average speed (mph)	11.24	11.22	13.93	18.38	n/a
Vehicle miles in passenger service (m)	279.2	74.2	47.9	23.4	424.7
Gross traffic receipts (£'000)	33,485	9,227	4,852	2,545	50,109
Total working expenses (£'000)	32,133	8,823	4,795	1,797	47,548
Net traffic receipts (£'000)	1,352	404	57	748	2,561
Advertising receipts etc (£'000)	458	120	75	0	653
Total net revenues*	1,810	525	132	748	3,215

* excludes central and capital charges

Source: Chambers Committee of Inquiry into London Transport, 1955. All prices are contemporary.

From Table 1, it is immediately clear that Country Buses and Coaches formed a relatively small part of the operation, with their combined numbers being less than Trolleybuses on their own in all the fields compared. Notably, though, Country Buses maintained a higher average speed than their Central London counterparts, and Coaches a good bit better still. However, given that British Transport Commission and capital charges are excluded, the financial position is clearly on the weak side.

Some further conclusions can be drawn, as shown in Table 2.

Table 2: London Transport 1953, statistical derivatives

	Central Buses	Trolleybuses	Country Buses	Coaches	All road operations
Vehicles as % of total	67.5%	17.7%	11.0%	3.8%	100%
Vehicle miles operated as % of total	65.7%	17.5%	11.3%	5.5%	100%
Vehicle miles per vehicle operated	42,671	43,240	44,850	62,903	43,788
Traffic receipts per vehicle operated	£5,118	£5,377	£4,543	£6,841	£5,166
Working expenses as % traffic receipts	96.0%	95.6%	98.8%	70.6%	94.9%
Working expenses per vehicle mile	11.5p	11.8p	10.0p	7.6p	11.2p

Table 2 shows that in terms of resources, Central Buses and Trolleybuses formed well over 80% of the operation, though when it comes to the use made of those vehicles, vehicle miles per vehicle operated, Country Buses were edging in front. As might be expected, Coaches were again doing much better, due at least in part to the nature of the operation.

However, on revenues per vehicle, Coaches did best and Country Buses worst. This reflected the lesser traffic potential in the more country areas, a problem which was not going to disappear. Thus the proportion of revenue eaten up by working expenses was highest for Country Buses, but only a little lower for Central Buses and Trolleybuses. The money-spinners (a relative term!) were Coaches, where the ratio of just over 70% was much more satisfactory.

Vehicle shortages in the 1970s were nothing new to London Country's predecessor. This is a Bristol K6A hired in by London Transport from Hants & Dorset in 1949 to make up numbers pending the receipt of new RTs. This is a lowbridge type on a 336 service from Chesham to Watford. *Ian Allan Library*

OUTSIDE COMPETITION

As the years progressed, the sanguine projections of earlier years turned out to be illusory. There were three main components of the falling passenger numbers.

The spread of television to increasing numbers of homes reduced the need to go out in the evenings to the cinema, dance hall, etc, which meant fewer passengers on the buses to get there and back again. Yet more significantly, the private car became increasingly dominant for local travel. This affected demand levels at all times of the day, the main exception at the time being the requirements for travel to and from school. A secondary and equally important effect was the resulting traffic congestion, which impinged equally on bus services, making the journey times slower and requiring more vehicles and staff to operate them, and in general making them less competitive. Thirdly, the improvement in railway services, particularly, but not solely, from electrification, offered fiercer competition, especially for Green Line coaches.

The first two were national phenomena rather than restricted to the Country Bus Area, but it is of interest to examine what happened on the railway.

RAILWAY COMPETITION

That the railways emerged from World War 2 in a battered state and with a huge maintenance backlog is not to be doubted, and it was some time before they found their feet again. Indeed, improvements only really came about with the Modernisation Plan of 1955, when the Government decided it was time to commit large-scale investment into their restoration and development.

This is not the place to discuss the merits of that policy, but it did have a considerable influence on public transport in the area. The main aspects are outlined here.

In the immediate postwar era, electric railway services covered most of the lines south of the Thames. To the north, electrification was the exception rather than the rule, with the dc line to Watford Junction being the main example. Electrification work progressed as follows:

1949	Liverpool Street-Shenfield
1960	Rickmansworth-Amersham and Chesham (London Underground)
1960	Liverpool Street-Bishop's Stortford and Hertford East
1962	Fenchurch Street-Upminster/Tilbury (and beyond)
1962	Sevenoaks-Tonbridge (and beyond)
1966	Euston-Tring (and beyond)
1976	Moorgate-Hertford North and Welwyn Garden City
1978	Welwyn Garden City-Hitchin/Royston
1983	St Pancras-Luton and beyond
1987	South Croydon-East Grinstead
1989	Watford Junction-St Albans Abbey

Very little of the area's rail network remained operated by diesel traction, essentially the lines from Paddington (other than to Heathrow) and Marylebone. The Redhill-Tonbridge line was electrified in 1994.

There were also a modest number of line and station openings:

1960	Edmonton Green-Cheshunt reopened, with three new stations
1966	Garston
1973	Stevenage station relocated half a mile south
1979	Hertford North-Stevenage reopened
1982	Watton-at-Stone
1982	Watford Stadium
1986	Welham Green
1988	How Wood

On the other hand, some rail services were withdrawn:

1951	Hertford-Hatfield-St Albans
1961	Dunton Green-Westerham
1964	St Margarets-Buntingford
1965	Hatfield-Welwyn Garden City-Luton-Dunstable
1967	Three Bridges-East Grinstead-Groombridge

In general terms, rail services were improved considerably with the advent of diesel traction but also large-scale electrification over what turned out to be many years. None of this helped the bus and coach services, the latter being particularly vulnerable. The advent of greater volumes of private cars and the resulting congestion, together with improvement in the competing railway, made radial Green Line routes in particular ever more difficult and thus more costly to operate.

THE ROUTEMASTER

The decision to develop the Routemaster bus in London came about mainly because of the need to replace the trolleybuses. 'While there is little to choose between the trolleybus and Routemaster in costs of operation, the trolleybus is at a disadvantage compared with the bus on other important grounds', said the 1957 Annual Report. The detailed reasons need not concern us here, but revolved around the lack of flexibility of a vehicle tied to a fixed power supply.

The standard Routemaster (RM) had 64 seats compared with the 56 of the RT, though on later, longer versions, when the legal restrictions on vehicle length had been relaxed, the RML incorporated an additional

The 'different' AEC Merlin, originally XMB1, then XMB15 and now MBS15, seen here on the 387 between Tring station and Tring. The station and an associated hotel are a full two miles from the centre of the small town. XMB15 was one of nine experimental Merlins allocated to the Country Area, though they were not used due to Union opposition. XMB1 was new in 1966, registered JLA 57D, and didn't enter service until 1969, by which time it had become XMB15 (SMM 15F) and was the only one of its kind in the Country Area. The others finished up as Central Buses on Red Arrow. *Ian Allan Library*

The 403 to Warlingham, operated here by Chelsham's RT3461 with the early winged device on the stairwell. This is Sanderstead Hill on 8 May 1976. *Guy Brigden*

AEC Swift SM534, new in June 1971, is at the head of a cavalcade of vehicles assembled to mark the opening of the Tonbridge bypass. *LCBS*

bay and seated 72. For Green Line coach operation, the prototype vehicle CRL4 was delivered in 1957; 'it has a high standard of comfort and is fitted with power-operated doors on the rear platform', enthused the 1957 Report.

Prototype Routemaster RM2 underwent trials in the Country Area in 1957 and was later joined by CRL4 (Coach Routemaster Leyland), which stayed. It was renumbered RMC4 on arrival of the 68 production coaches, RMC1453-1520, in 1962. Initial use was on Green Line routes 715/715A, their first regular use of double-deckers. These were followed up in 1965 by the longer version, the RCL. These formed a fleet of 43 coaches, RCL2218-60, which were allocated to the Green Line services from Essex to Aldgate.

The bus versions, the 100 72-seat RMLs, arrived in two batches — RML2306-55, 2411-60 during 1965/66. First examples went to Godstone for conversion of the 409/410/411 group of routes and a number of Central Area red RMLs had to be borrowed initially to make up the necessary numbers.

Deliveries of the new fleet to the Country Bus & Coach department eventually totalled 209 vehicles. Whatever the advantages of the Routemaster, operation by a driver only was completely out of the question. That such vehicles should have been delivered for country work as late as 1966 suggests that London Transport's appreciation of the increasingly dire economic situation in which its services were operating was seriously at odds with reality.

HERBERT COMMISSION

In 1957, the Herbert Commission was appointed to examine the structure of local government in London, and its broad conclusions were accepted by the Government.

As a result, the Greater London Council was established in 1965 under powers given in the Local Government Act 1963. The Commission's remit, however, had excluded any consideration of the division of responsibility for public transport services. The ultimate responsibility for what were by then the London Transport Board and the British Railways Board thus remained with the Minister of Transport.

This was clearly a major limitation on the GLC's ability to act as a strategic planning body for the whole of the London area, and in particular its ability to develop comprehensive plans covering all forms of transport. Further change was to come, but not for some years yet.

THE GATHERING STORM

It is a gross exaggeration to suggest that the 1958 London Bus Strike was the root cause of the severe and continuing reduction of passenger numbers which was to be the hallmark of the 1960s, but it certainly didn't help. In those far-off days, a wage claim by the Transport & General Workers Union was rejected by the Executive as excessive. It was referred to the Industrial Court, who found in favour of a much lower figure for some staff and against the claim altogether for others. Here it is merely recorded that the findings were rejected by the Union and an all-out bus strike was called. In the event this lasted from 5 May until 21 June 1958, during which time the stoppage was total. London Transport's Underground services continued to operate normally.

The decline in passenger journeys on Country Bus & Coach is illustrated below.

Country Bus & Coach, passenger journeys (millions)
selected years

Year	1955	1958	1960	1963	1966	1969
Country Bus	297	218	250	231	200	177
Green Line	35	30	36	30	25	21
Total	332	248	286	261	225	198

Source: Annual Report and Accounts, year concerned

Clearly such results could not continue indefinitely, and a concomitant result was the reining back of the mileage operated to reduce costs. But this, too, is a double-edged sword. Lower mileage means a less comprehensive service offered to the public; from what has already been said it will not be surprising to find that evenings were an early target for reductions. Some vehicle operating costs will be saved, perhaps equal to or more than the direct loss of revenue. However, if the vehicle itself is still needed for the peak, it isn't possible to save the costs of providing, maintaining, insuring and garaging it. Practical considerations as well as staff agreements will determine the extent to which crew costs can be saved.

There is also a further effect, in that the overall service becomes just that little bit less attractive to the passenger, and the incentive to buy a car is also boosted to the same extent.

Such arguments can be taken too far, since there are various ways to cut costs, but the incipient problem will remain if traffic is being lost. It proved difficult for Country Bus & Coach to cut costs through reductions in mileage operated as fast as traffic was falling, and this had the result that the average vehicle gradually grew emptier and emptier. This is illustrated in the table following, which shows the average occupancy:

Country Bus & Coach, passenger miles per vehicle mile
selected years

Year	1956	1960	1964	1968
Country Bus	15.9	15.2	13.7	12.9
Green Line	15.8	16.0	13.2	12.2

Source: Annual Report and Accounts, year concerned

As can be seen, Green Line traffic kept up better than bus until the early 1960s.

FINANCIAL PERFORMANCE

How well were the undertakings performing, financially? This alarming table gives the answer, though the source is unclear as to whether it represents the whole operation or only the least satisfactory part of it. Either way, it shows how early severe problems were developing, but also that Green Line was, comparatively, the

A classic Routemaster coach duty sees RMC1490 on a 718 working from Harlow to Windsor passing the Hilton Hotel in Park Lane.
AEC/Ian Allan Library

best performing part of the operation. Single-deck Country Bus operation on Sundays was the worst, but double-deck was almost as bad, as was also the single-deck operation during the week.

Proportion of vehicles on unremunerative routes, as a percentage of total vehicles operating given groups of routes. Results of a representative summer week, 1964.

| | Country bus | | Green Line Coach | |
	Double-deck	Single-deck	Double-deck	Single-deck
Monday-Friday	46%	89%	31%	35%
Saturday	15%	68%	7%	-
Sunday	86%	100%	11%	13%

Source: London Transport Board, evidence to the Select Committee on Nationalised Industries 1965, London Transport. 313-1, Appendix 31

To the table, the notes add blithely that 'this shows a better out-turn than a winter week at weekends, particularly on Sundays when traffic receipts are more vulnerable to the weather'.

In any event, many bus routes were discontinued by Country Bus & Coach, sometimes for a new future under another operator. In rural Surrey, route 448 Guildford-Ewhurst was acquired by independent Tillingbourne in 1963. Five years later, London Transport withdrew the 433 to Coldharbour, which was replaced without subsidy by a Royal Mail Post Bus.

THE JACK COMMITTEE

Similar problems were being recorded nationwide, particularly in the more rural parts of Britain. The area served by the Country Buses could hardly be described as really rural, but neither was much of it densely built-up. If one word has to be used to describe it, that word is 'suburban'. In the latter part of the 20th century, the suburban concept was not one which excited the academic researchers, as later events demonstrated. The key words then were 'urban' and 'rural'.

Nevertheless, there was a sizeable element of the operation which might genuinely attract the rural label. The upshot had been the earlier commissioning by the Minister of Transport of a report, 'Rural Bus Services', which was published in 1961. This was the findings of a Committee chaired by Professor Jack, by whose name the report is generally known. Its task was 'to review present (1958) trends in rural bus services and in particular to enquire into the adequacy of those services; to consider possible methods of ensuring adequate services in future; and to make recommendations'.

This was in the days when public transport was expected to be wholly commercial, and the concept of Government subvention (other than under duress as in the case of bodies like the nationalised British Railways) was not generally recognised. The bus industry was one which had consistently managed to run profitably since its inception, why could it not continue to do so? The Jack Report was however uncompromising in its conclusions and recommendations, the main ones of which were as follows:

- The prime cause of the rural bus problem is the growth in private transport
- The problem involves hardship to a small number of people and inconvenience to more, which does not accord well with any reasonable concept of service adequacy
- Any solution involving financial assistance should relate to the circumstances of each case
- The Postmaster General should consider the possibility of allowing fare-paying passengers to travel in Post Office vans
- Adequate rural bus services cannot be provided except as a result of some measure of financial assistance from outside the industry
- Relief of fuel tax would be simple, but would be imprecise and indiscriminate
- Of the various ways in which financial assistance might be given, administration through the County Councils would be the most satisfactory
- The cost should fall partly on the County Councils and partly on the Exchequer.

However, in the event, weightier matters were on the Government's mind, and less that two years later, in spring 1963, 'The Reshaping of British Railways', the first report from the hand of Dr Richard (later Lord) Beeching as Chairman of the newly formed British Railways Board was published. Several years thus elapsed with little action, the exception being Fuel Duty Rebate (now know as Bus Service Operator's Grant), which was introduced under the Finance Act 1965.

LONDON TRANSPORT RESULTS

One of the discouraging elements of the London Transport operation in the 1960s was the level of capital spending on renewal, replacement and improvements. Discounting new railways, such spending was around half that required for the whole of the 1950s, and similarly for the latter part of the 1960s. In 1970, the Prices & Incomes Board commented as follows:

> 'From the end of the war until 1969, London Transport's capital spending on essential renewal and replacement of physical assets was lower than required to maintain an appropriate level of comfort, reliability and convenience for passengers. The main reason for this was that the level of fares was too low and at times artificially depressed as a matter of national policy. This situation was to some extent concealed by the policy whereby assets were depreciated on an historic cost (rather than a replacement cost) basis.'

While the majority of such spending was likely to be on the Underground (the figures provided do not differentiate), it was a poor omen for the state of the bus fleets.

TRANSPORT ACT 1968

A change of Government and the appointment of the redoubtable Mrs Barbara (later Lady) Castle as Minister of Transport heralded what became the far-reaching Transport Act 1968.

This wide-ranging piece of legislation resulted in many organisational changes, including, for instance,

RMCs were later demoted to bus work, but retained their doors. This is Dartford's RMC1462 on a 499 bearing a rather unhelpful destination blind on 16 July 1977. It carries the monochrome version of the NBC logo in front of the company name on the side. *Guy Brigden*

the setting up of the Passenger Transport Executives (PTEs) and their controlling elected authorities in the Metropolitan areas of the country. Eventually local bus and rail services were brought together in seven areas in a form which offered direction, finance and control to public bodies. The former municipal bus fleets, and some others, which operated in these areas became wholly owned subsidiaries of the PTEs.

General help for the bus industry contained in the Transport Act 1968 was the introduction of new bus grant for approved vehicles, under which the Minister provided a grant at 25% (later 50%) of the capital cost to bus companies. The aim was to speed the move to one-man operation, as it was then termed.

The Fuel Duty Rebate payments to the bus industry by Government were virtually doubled, and the Minister also took note of the Jack Report of 1961 on rural bus services. This is considered further in Chapter 4.

NATIONAL BUS COMPANY

The Act also set up the publicly owned National Bus Company (NBC), the constituents of which were the bus companies which were formerly part of the Transport Holding Company (THC), itself set up under the Transport Act 1962. These were the territorial (as opposed to the municipal) bus companies, a combination of the Tilling and BET groups. The former were wholly owned by the THC and thus fully nationalised; the BET Group companies were then part owned.

NBC was created on 1 January 1969 with 54 subsidiary operating companies, and was given the statutory duty to conduct its business 'so as to secure that its revenue was not less than sufficient for making provision for the meeting of charges properly chargeable to revenue, taking one year with another'. In other words, this was a straight commercial remit, save only the benefits that the NBC might derive from the three external revenue sources of new bus grant, Fuel Duty Rebate and those new-fangled local authority grants.

Provision was however made for the Government to make capital grants for major improvements, and the 1967 White Paper mentioned specifically bus stations and depots, and interchanges. The 1968 Act made clear that these, the so-called Section 56 grants, would be payable only for projects which were in accordance with the local authority's general transport planning for the area.

NBC had wide-ranging powers as might be expected for any bus company, including for instance the ability to carry passengers' luggage and act as travel agents. There was also a mutual duty of co-operation with both the London Transport Board and the British Railways Board for the purpose of co-ordinating passenger transport services and to exchange information as necessary. This duty was extended to the PTEs where they existed, but not to the local authorities who might provide the rural bus grants; their role was still seen as largely peripheral.

As to NBC itself, it 'is being established to make easier the reorganisation of bus services to meet the needs of each area. It will not be a centralised board but in effect a holding company owning a large number of local subsidiaries which will be responsive to local conditions and problems and will co-operate closely with the communities they serve... In short, the establishment of the NBC will provide a sound basis for developing on a rational basis the provision of bus services throughout England and Wales.' Thus were the sentiments expressed in the Government's White Paper 'Public Transport and Traffic', in 1967.

FURTHER REORGANISATION

Comprehensive as the 1968 Act was, with its 281 pages, there was still some unfinished business. This was in London, where the Government decided to transfer the operations of London Transport to the Greater London Council (GLC), itself created in 1965. In essence, the Government now believed that local transport was a local rather than a national concern, and the GLC was the ideal body to take on this task.

Thus the position of the GLC was to be strengthened 'to develop policies and to encourage, organise and where appropriate to carry out measures, which will promote the provision of integrated, efficient and economic transport facilities and services for Greater London'.

Ideal within London it might be, but such a concept did not sit well with the very extensive part of the London Transport operation outside the GLC area. That would amount to political control of services over a wide swathe of territory resting with a remote body, whose electorate did not include this larger area. Division of the London Transport Board's empire was thus proposed, to take effect as follows:

- Central Buses, running largely within Greater London, would be transferred to the new Executive
- Country Buses, which operated largely outside Greater London, and the Green Line coach services, which operated from the same garages, would be transferred to the National Bus Company
- The Underground would be taken over by the Executive, and this would include those sections outside Greater London in Hertfordshire, Buckinghamshire and Essex
- The London Passenger Transport Area and the London Special Area, in which London Transport had special privileges, would be abolished
- Within Greater London, the new Executive would be free to operate the stage-carriage (local) and express bus services they wished. Other operators (including the NBC and its subsidiaries) would be allowed to run such services only under consents from or agreements with the Executive
- For stage and express services which crossed the GLC boundary or ran wholly outside it, all operators including the LTE would require a Road Service Licence from the Traffic Commissioners
- Fares on services within Greater London would be determined by the GLC, but outside Greater London by the Traffic Commissioners
- The Executive would be under a duty to ensure that its revenue from all sources was sufficient to meet the financial objectives agreed with the GLC, which was substantially less onerous than the commercial remit of the National Bus Company to which Country Buses and Green Line would be transferred
- The National Bus Company would assume part of the capital debt of the Board.

The above is condensed from the Transport in London White Paper of July 1968. And so it came to pass. This major reorganisation came into effect with the Transport (London) Act 1969, and the new arrangements became fully effective on 1 January 1970.

IMPLICATIONS

The overall effect was that the situation outside the Greater London boundary would become similar to the situation elsewhere in Britain since the 1930s, but that the curtailed London Transport's operation would retain monopoly powers within Greater London.

So far, so good, but there were sizeable implications for bus services crossing the GLC boundary. Those emanating from outside would be expected to be profitable and thus able to stand on their own commercial feet; that any might benefit from the rural bus grant provisions of the Act a year previously was at best unlikely. They could however only cross the Greater London boundary with the agreement of London Transport, and there they would operate a fares policy in accordance with the wishes of LT and run such services as it might consider necessary.

For London Transport (formerly Central Bus) services which, almost by definition, originated from inside the Greater London boundary, the reverse was largely true, though there was no requirement as such to charge commercial fares if the Greater London Council was content for them not to do so. Thus while it was up to the GLC to determine LT's financial objectives, there was no suggestion that the county portions of those services would be subsidised from Greater London Council funds, either directly or via London Transport. Given the situation as described earlier here, the likelihood that fares might rise substantially was strong.

Similarly, the effects on what was to become London Country Bus Services Ltd as a constituent of the National Bus Company were also uncertain. While they would be supported for the portions of their routes which continued to operate within the GLC boundary, what would happen outside? Here there were some truly rural routes in a rural bus grant sense, but these were only of minor importance compared with the operation as a whole. Again, fares rises were perhaps the least unacceptable of the likely evils to come.

The above is written with the huge advantage of hindsight; what actually transpired will be discussed in the chapters to come.

Above: The shortcoming of the Routemaster and its double-deck predecessors was the inability to be adapted in any conceivable way for operation by the driver only. This was later to become a concern on safety grounds as well as access difficulties. RML2411 works a 407 at Langley, Berks, on 12 April 1978. *Guy Brigden*

Left: Race days at Ascot are usually thought of as relatively high-class affairs. This is a 701 Green Line Relief using Leatherhead's RT3665 on 20 June 1974. It appears to have been parked along with all the other spectator vehicles. *Guy Brigden*

3   London Country established

'Running buses is a tough job, but very rewarding and great fun.'

Geoffrey Fernyhough, General Manager London Country, 1972

In the deadpan manner beloved of such documents, the National Bus Company (NBC) Annual Report of 1970 recorded as follows:

'Under the Transport (London) Act 1969, those parts of the London Transport Board's undertaking known as country buses and coaches were, from 1 January 1970, vested in London Country Bus Services Ltd (LCBS) as a new subsidiary of the National Bus Company.'

Somehow, this did not accord with popular notions of an effusive welcome, but then NBC was well aware of what it was taking on. NBC itself was precisely a year old when it had to absorb its London outcast.

Under the provisions of the Transport (London) Act 1969, the Country Bus & Coach Department of the then London Transport Board was to be transferred to a new company formed for the purpose, which would become a wholly owned subsidiary of the National Bus Company. At the same time, the whole of the capital debt of the London Transport Board was to be written off by the Ministry of Transport as at midnight on 31 December 1969.

The transfer of the Country Bus & Coach Department to the new NBC subsidiary included all property rights and liabilities and the new company was to be known as London Country Bus Services Ltd (LCBS). The vesting day was 1 January 1970. LCBS was incorporated on 9 October 1968, but remained non-operational until then.

So far, so good, but the financial arrangements on transfer were far from what the new company might have wished. This is how London Country itself described the situation a few years later, in 1974:

'On Vesting Day, no depreciation reserves or replacement provisions were available to the new Company, although these stood in the books of the London Transport Board at £5,500,000. This is significantly important as, during the years 1968 and 1969, the fleet of vehicles and buildings had been allowed to deteriorate. For example, the average age of the fleet was 18.4 years.

'On 26 August 1969, the Chairman of the National Bus Company had written to the Minister of Transport stressing the financial need of the new Company. From figures produced by London Transport, the Country Bus & Coach Department had operated at a loss of £988,000 in 1968 and some £555,000 in 1969.

'On 19 January 1970, the Minister of Transport in the House of Commons, when referring to the National Bus Company's financial target, said "I have made specific allowance for the estimated loss of £600,000 in 1970 and £500,000 in 1971 of the subsidiary company to which the London Country Bus and Green Line services have been transferred.

'No financial assistance, apart from grants by local authorities under s34 of the Transport Act 1968, has been provided to meet the Company's losses and urgent capital requirements. In fact, the Company commenced trading on 1 January 1970 with no bank balance and a mere sum of £2,500 in the form of petty cash floats.

'A total of 565 new vehicles were brought into the fleet from 1970-73 and its average age was reduced to 10 years.

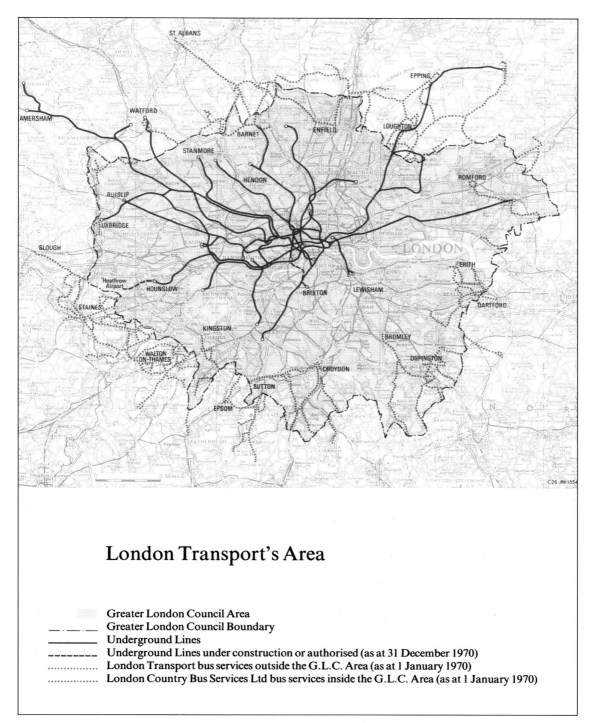

London Transport's Area

                  Greater London Council Area
— · — · —   Greater London Council Boundary
─────────   Underground Lines
─ ─ ─ ─ ─   Underground Lines under construction or authorised (as at 31 December 1970)
·············   London Transport bus services outside the G.L.C. Area (as at 1 January 1970)
·············   London Country Bus Services Ltd bus services inside the G.L.C. Area (as at 1 January 1970)

London Transport's area as redefined in 1970, in a map which shows the extent to which the red buses then pushed out into the out-counties, but also how far Country Buses extended into Greater London. Green Line services are not shown, only the Underground which penetrated Hertfordshire, Buckinghamshire and Essex. *Author's collection*

Above: RT4117, by now in London Country livery with canary yellow band, toils up the modest hill in Ewell village on a 406 Kingston-Tadworth service. Their advancing years were by this time — around 1975 — becoming only too obvious. *John Glover*

Below: This SMW is seen in St Albans on service 343 to Welham Green, part of the additional help brought in from outside the company, in this case from South Wales Transport. *Barry Le Jeune*

'The company commenced without a head office or central workshops. The old East Surrey Traction Company offices at Reigate were taken over from the London Transport Board and an extension to the building was completed in 1972 at a cost of £120,000 to house the Head Office Administration.

'Numerous garage and workshop improvements were undertaken in these initial years at the 28 garages. However, the Company was not able to acquire suitable premises for central workshops, although negotiations (ultimately successful) were proceeding with the New Towns Commissioner at Crawley.

'As at the beginning of 1974, London Country operated some 1,150 buses and coaches and employed 5,000 staff. The network of Country and Green Line services operated in the following local authority areas:

- Greater London
- Surrey
- Kent
- Hertfordshire
- Essex
- Buckinghamshire
- Berkshire
- Bedfordshire
- East Sussex
- West Sussex'

Finally, with just a mere hint of bravado, 'the National Bus Company is the largest single bus organisation in the United Kingdom, and London Country is one of its largest subsidiary companies'. The last was certainly a fair claim, since the LCBS fleet accounted for nearly 6% of the total buses owned by NBC subsidiaries.

The Company's own analysis of its situation was thus somewhat uncomfortable reading, from which a number of conclusions might be drawn.

- First, whatever the rights and wrongs of the matter, the transfer from London Transport had not addressed a number of issues. These would result in long-term problems
- The asset base of London Country was just about adequate for the time being, but many matters would have to be resolved in the not-too-far-distant future
- Cost recovery through fares on the services then operated was insufficient to meet the company's financial needs as specified by the National Bus Company, without external help
- That any such assistance, rather than from a single London Transport parent company, would in future have to come from the ten local authorities listed above.

For, although London Country was in many respects a very large bus company, in some elements there were serious shortcomings. Thus:

- There were initially no headquarters offices (see above) and the Central Services element of the London Transport organisation was no longer available to the company
- There were no overhaul workshops, reliance for such work in the past having been placed with those of Central Buses at Chiswick and Aldenham as part of London Transport
- The vehicles in the fleet as transferred were nearly all to London Transport design and specifications, to whose resources London Country was obliged to resort for spares
- Bus operation by driver only was not a physical possibility with a large proportion of the double-deck vehicles in particular, though the fleet was ageing and this could be corrected in replacements
- The company inherited pay rates and labour agreements which were, from a company viewpoint, rather more onerous than it might wish, and certainly more so than those of adjacent NBC subsidiaries
- The operating area surrounding London with a ring of services but with a large gap in the middle, itself traversed by the company's own coach services, was not an easy one to manage

- The company's services which operated into and out of the Greater London area, together with the fares to be charged and the associated conditions of travel, were to a large extent specified for them by London Transport
- Most seriously of all, perhaps, the commercial market for London Country's bus and coach services appeared to be in long-term decline.

FLEET INHERITANCE

First, the fleet with which the company had to provide the services it offered to the public. Following transfer in 1970, the company was to own 1,267 vehicles, 721 of them double-deck and 546 single-deck. The fleet composition was as follows:

Double-deck Vehicles

Built	Type	No	Description	Last used
1948-54	RT	484	AEC Regent III	1978
1952	RLH	17	AEC Regent III lowbridge	1970
1957, 1962	RMC	69	Routemaster coaches (27ft 6in)	1980
1965	RCL	43	Routemaster coaches (30ft)	1979
1965	XF	8	Daimler Fleetline	1981
1965-66	RML	97	Routemaster buses (30ft)	1980
1966	XA	3	Leyland Atlantean	1973

Single-deck Vehicles

Built	Type	No	Description	Last used
1951-53	RF	413	AEC Regal	1979
1953-54	GS	10	Guy Special	1972
1965	RC	14	AEC Reliance coach	1977
1966	XMB	1	AEC Merlin	1973
1968	MB	33	AEC Merlin	1980
1968	MBS	75	AEC Merlin	1980

The unsatisfactory nature of the fleet is immediately apparent. Its largest single component, the 484 RTs, were by then a minimum of 16 years old, while the 413 RFs were even older. The latter, which were built for either bus or Green Line work, had already covered a million miles each when refurbished in the late 1960s. It was these vehicles, together with the 17 lowbridge double-deckers (RLH) and the 10 small single-deckers (GS), together accounting for 73% of the total fleet, which were largely responsible for its high average age. NBC regarded the useful life of a bus as between six and 12 years, way below the 18.4 years average of the then LCBS fleet.

What else was there? The Routemasters, splendid vehicles though in many ways they were, enforced crew operation by their design. That left just 11 modern (in the sense of driver-only-operable) double-deckers in the form of Atlanteans and Fleetlines; the X prefix to the names stood for eXperimental. No wonder bus grant was introduced nationally by the Government to aid fleet modernisation, something of which LCBS was to make full use.

Apart from the 14 AEC Reliance coaches of 1965, that left only the AEC Merlins which, if nothing else, were at least of recent construction. They were ordered by London Transport, in part to implement its own Bus Reshaping Plan of 1966. New shorter routes were to replace longer ones, often using buses with high standing capacity (the MBS version). They were not popular vehicles and posed significant engineering problems.

Of the RTs, 34 were sold back to London Transport in September 1972, but the last was not withdrawn from LCBS service until 1978. On the formation of London Country, three green RMLs were exchanged with LT for the three red XA Atlanteans shown, although these later joined the other XAs in Hong Kong. Thus London Country inherited a fleet of 209 Routemasters, all confined to bus work after the last double-deck

New one-man-operable double-deckers were vital to London Country's survival, and while Atlanteans came to be the saviours of the double-deck fleet, the process was started by a few Daimler Fleetlines. Here, in early London Country livery, AF8 is reaching the summit south of Redhill on the occasion of the London Brighton Historic Commercial Vehicles rally, held on the first Sunday in May. *John Glover*

Green Line route, Godstone's 709, was converted to one-man in 1975. The former coach fleet was all redundant by the end of 1977, though the RMLs continued in use for the time being. Many Routemasters found their way back to LT over the years.

The last conductor operation took place on 14 March 1981 with the conversion of the 477 route at Swanley. Routemaster use had ceased the previous year, but for the time being the new replacement Atlanteans were crew operated.

By 1970, many of the GSs had already found service with other operators, Tillingbourne Valley in particular, and over half of the original fleet survived into preservation.

A NEW FLEET

As will be clear from the table, the former LT designs were all disposed of during the ensuing decade. That presaged a very considerable fleet replacement effort, in the course of which London Country gradually acquired vehicles of the same designs as any other NBC company. There was however one matter still to be resolved, and that was the 138 AEC Swifts, the shorter version of the Merlin, which had been ordered by London Transport but not delivered until after the split. These met with a similar fate to the Merlins proper, and all had gone by 1981.

Of the new double-deck vehicles, a brief flurry of 11 Fleetlines (AF) was followed with a long-term acquisition of what in the end came to 293 Leyland Atlanteans (AN) delivered from 1972 to 1981. These were succeeded by 75 Leyland Olympians (LR) by the end of double-deck acquisitions by LCBS in 1985, and there were also 15 Olympian coaches (LRC) for Green Line. In between, 1977 saw the acquisition of 15 Bristol VRTs (BT), though these lasted only four years in LCBS ownership.

On the single-deck side, 90 AEC Reliances (RP) were ordered for wholesale Green Line coach work, and

Left: A mixture of vehicles at Harlow bus station in June 1975 with RT3816 on the 339, carrying corporate advertising extolling the virtues of the National Bus Company, in the foreground, and an RP and an AN behind. *Barry Le Jeune*

Below: Leatherhead's SM110 in Leatherhead on the 418 to Bookham station when new in July 1970. *Barry Le Jeune*

another 36 AEC Swifts (21 SMA, 15 SMW) were diverted from an order placed by NBC sister company South Wales Transport. All these were delivered to London Country by 1972. This year also saw the arrival of the first of the all-conquering single-deck vehicle of the 1970s, the Leyland National.

The Leyland Nationals were welcomed by LCBS; the following is derived from contemporary company sources. 'Leyland National, bus of the future', enthused London Country's staff magazine in late 1972. How was this vehicle seen when it was introduced, well over 30 years ago?

'London Country is one of the first companies in Britain to take delivery of the Leyland National — a single-deck bus built only after considerable research into the requirements of passengers, drivers and operators. Our first two have been prepared in the livery of Superbus in Stevenage. Others are destined for Green Line work, where they will assist in the replacement of the now ageing RF coaches.

'Our Leyland Nationals are 11.3m in length' (later, 10.3m versions were also bought), 'having been designed and built by a joint organisation controlled by British Leyland and the National Bus Company. They have been designed with one man operation in mind and a spacious and well lit front entrance will offer an easier and safer journey for many elderly passengers.'

Design

'All well-established principles of vehicle design, building and performance were carefully evaluated. Needs of users have never before been so carefully studied or so exactly translated into vehicle design and performance. The final plans allow for integral construction. This means there is no separate chassis and body (rather like a Routemaster) and it is immensely safe structurally. Repairs and maintenance are unusually simple. Air suspension of an advanced and reliable design is provided.'

Passenger appeal

'The smooth ride is far in advance of any other bus. Noise and vibration is down to an insignificant level and no longer is there any 'lurching or jerking'. The outside appearance of the bus is unusual because the rear 'hump' houses a fully automatic temperature control with warm air curtains across the doors to prevent cold air entering.'

Driver appeal

'Major changes see controls grouped into four categories:

1. Driver controls — wipers, washers, lights etc.
2. Prepare to drive controls — gear selection, parking brake etc.
3. Fare collection equipment.
4. Passenger comfort controls — lighting, heating.

The positioning of these control groups is based on priority of use and, for instance, the least used (group 4) are furthest away from the driver.' (It didn't actually say that they were the least important, too, but it was a close thing.)

Power

'Like other new single-deck vehicles, the engine is placed at the rear, but is the recently introduced supercharged 200bhp 8.2litre 500 series Leyland fixed head engine. From a maintenance point of view, the engine has three distinct advantages — accessible running units, common components and easy fault location.' Automatic transmission and two-pedal control were supplied.

Passenger dream bus

'There are other new features which go to make the almost perfect bus and over the next few months many garages will receive batches of these vehicles. They have undergone the most exhaustive research and road testing programme ever designed for a passenger vehicle. We are confident that passengers and staff will benefit.'

Were they liked by the public? The Leyland Nationals certainly had a low floor as far as the step up beyond the centre exit (where fitted), and that was a plus point. But the green and white external livery was not becoming, while inside the dark green shiny vinyl seats and generally stark finish was not welcomed by those used to the comfort of London Transport moquette. London Country effectively had little choice, given its precarious financial position on the one hand and NBC corporate control on the other. It was, however, somewhat of a relief when the later short versions (the SNBs) indeed adopted moquette seating.

London Country took delivery of 543 Leyland Nationals between 1972 and 1979. The first 70 were of the 'long' 11.3m variety, the rest 10.3m; the latter proved much more versatile in negotiating the roads 'that only a Country Bus might go'. Some were finished to coach specification with (sometimes rather theoretically) upgraded seating, and were designated LNC or SNC for the shorter ones; the corresponding buses were LNB and SNB. All the long Nationals had been withdrawn by the time of deregulation in 1985. The original deliveries, the LNs, were the only dual-door versions in the fleet; generally, the separation of boarding and alighting flows was not an important issue in London Country's operation. Two sets of doors meant lost seating space, was the source of draughts in the saloon and was one

Left: Whether the full National Bus regalia ever suited the RTs is a matter of debate. RT604 is now a preserved vehicle, photographed in Dorking in September 2005. *John Glover*

Below: One of the Metro-Scanias on Superbus service in Stevenage bus station in August 1971. *Barry Le Jeune*

more item to maintain.

This still left a hole at the bottom of the market, for which some Bristol LHSs were acquired between 1973 and 1977. There were two varieties, the 8ft wide BL totalling 23 and the 7ft 8in wide BN type of which there were 44. These too were economy vehicles in appearance, comfort and quality of ride. The nadir was to find a BN turn up on Green Line duties, from which it was abundantly clear that the N stood for nasty. More seriously, though, they had only 35 seats; while this was adequate for much of the day on many rural routes, it was a substantial constraint when the carriage of schoolchildren was required.

Other LCBS single-deck bus types were the MS Metro-Scanias (1971, total four), FT Ford Transits (1974, total five), and the MBM Mercedes 608Ds (1986, total 12).

That gave a total of 394 new double-deck vehicles and 880 single-deckers, or 1,264 buses, excluding coaches, which will be considered separately, acquired new over nearly 17 years. Overall, 565 new vehicles were taken into the fleet between 1970 and 1973, bringing the average fleet age down to 10 years. It might have been enough, though in the event much use had to be made of hiring-in from elsewhere and the purchase of such secondhand vehicles as could be found. But that was still a little way into the future.

An analysis of changes in the London Country fleet carried out by Hertfordshire in 1977, 1980 and 1983 showed that in 1977 there was still a substantial number of former London Transport vehicles, but these had all but gone by 1980. After that date, when the new bus grant was progressively reduced until it was discontinued in 1984, new vehicle deliveries dropped away. As a result, the average vehicle age in the London Country fleet, 6.5 years in 1977 and a low of 4.3 years in 1980, rose to 5.6 years in 1983.

While the total vehicles in the fleet at a little more than 1,100 remained relatively constant, the numbers of coaches rose very substantially from 37 in 1977 to 249 in 1983. Dual-purpose vehicles such as the RPs and SNCs were counted as buses. The number of double-decker buses reduced slightly over the period.

LIVERIES

Early changes saw the introduction of the winged wheel. This was designed in conjunction with the Publicity Department of the National Bus Company and represented the green ring around London, with a wheel and movement on the road. 'The angled bars give depth and perspective to the symbol, which gives the feeling of transport amidst green countryside', or so it was said. It was usually referred to, not unreasonably, as the Flying Polo.

The next move was to brighten up the fleet but still using the traditional Lincoln green. From 1970 deliveries of new vehicles and others which had been modernised were given a relieving band of canary yellow. The cream lining was retained on the older vehicles, specifically the RT, RF and GS types, all of which were due for gradual withdrawal over the next few years, and the two-tone green livery for Green Line remained unaltered.

Routemasters and other non-new vehicles started to appear in the standard NBC light green livery in 1972. Its appeal is largely a matter of opinion, but LCBS management clearly preferred the traditional and much darker Lincoln green. In the mid-1980s the white band on several buses was overpainted in a brighter green.

GARAGES

At the inception of London Country, there were 29 garages, all but one (Romford) in the Home Counties. Two were opened by the company, one at Slough on a new site, the other at Crawley as replacement premises. The inadequacies of many of the premises in modern terms were one of the reasons for the maintenance problems experienced in the early days.

Each garage was allocated a code (see Appendix B) carried on each side of the vehicles, originally by means of a stencil secured in brackets provided for the purpose; it was supplemented by a second stencil showing the vehicle running number — the duty it was undertaking. In this way, the identity of a vehicle in terms of the garage at which it was based and what it was supposed to be doing could easily be ascertained by roadside staff. Later, the garage stencils were replaced by letters painted white in the same position.

To give some idea of the work of a garage, in 1983 Hertford operated 50 vehicles, 19 double-deck buses, 19 single-deck buses and 12 Green Line coaches. The garage operated 18 bus and two Green Line routes; the shortest was the 333 (2.6 miles), the longest was the 798, operated jointly with Eastern Counties, from London to Cambridge, 57 miles. Each week, 42,550 scheduled miles were run, 29,700 on bus routes and 12,850 on the coach services. Additional miles were often run to duplicate busy services, and also at weekends on rail replacement services when there was engineering work on the railways.

A total of 106 drivers was employed at Hertford and there were 44 engineering staff, all of whom worked shifts to help keep the vehicles on the road 18½ hours a day, 363 days a year. On weekdays services started at 05.43 and continued until 00.15, a little less on Sundays. No services operated on Christmas Day or Boxing Day, but these were the only exceptions.

The whole was overseen by the Garage Traffic Superintendent and the Garage Engineering Superintendent.

TESTING

As well as being a normal London Country operating garage, Hertford was the home of three special back-up functions for bus services more generally.

Buses were hired from London Transport at various times, such as Merlin MBS70, bound for Guildford on the 425 in February 1976.
Barry Le Jeune

First, there was the PSV testing station, where the Ministry tested buses and coaches. This was a consequence of the post-1980 legislation, which required every vehicle to be tested annually at an approved site. Overhauls were still carried out every six to seven years, but intermediate servicing needed to be of a high standard to meet the test demands.

Once a bus had passed its first test, it would receive a 'Certificate of Fitness' and would then have to be retested on or before the same date the following year. The programme of initial tests had to be spaced out so that garages had an even flow of vehicles coming up for test.

Vehicles tested at Hertford were not just those from the garage, but from the whole of London Country's North East area. This comprised Harlow, Hatfield, Hertford, St Albans and Stevenage garages. The test station facility was also available for other operators, since while it was in use, it was deemed to be the property of the Department of Transport.

Other LCBS test stations were at Reigate, Northfleet and Watford. Each was equipped with an inspection pit or lift, jacking equipment, a headlamp-setting meter, a roller brake tester, 'shaker plates' to test kingpin wear, microphone communication between the examiner and driver when inspecting underneath the vehicle, and suitable office space for the examiner.

The actual test took about an hour, including checks on noise and smoke emission, correct functioning of all electrical and air-operated equipment, condition of steering, brakes and tyres, and the accuracy of tachographs, if fitted.

Other facilities at Hertford were the Area Stores, which supplied the whole of London Country's Northern Division (North East and North West Areas), covering territory from Bishop's Stortford to Windsor. There was a Southern Division stores at Reigate, and both Hertford and Reigate stores were supplied from Crawley Works. The supply of parts was computer controlled, and visual display units were used to speed information flows.

Hertford was also the home of Tyre Stores, which supplied tyres to London Country vehicles at all garages.

PRODUCTION WOES

Nationally, the bus industry entered what proved to be an extremely difficult period as the 1970s progressed. The key problem was the shortage of spare parts needed to maintain vehicles, but this was coupled with a seeming inability to deliver new vehicles as well. As a result, many buses had to be taken off the road as unserviceable, resulting in much lost mileage.

London Country was harder hit than many other companies, since its fleet at this stage was still largely that obtained from London Transport at the time of the handover. A number of factors contributed to the situation that developed:

- London Transport's ending of the arrangement for the overhaul of units
- Backlog of work caused by staff shortages
- More than 20 different types of bus operated
- Insufficient repair facilities, particularly the lack of a central repair facility.

The combination made London Country's position precarious in the extreme. The results were little short of disastrous; on 1 October 1974, the position was as follows:

- Total fleet owned, buses and coaches   1,200
- Of which, required for service   986
- Vehicles under repair, or awaiting spares or maintenance   347
- Vehicles available   853
- Number of vehicle duties not covered   133

The fleet was thus 13% below strength, which translated into 13,800 miles not operated. Everything which could be pressed into service was, and planned withdrawals ceased. The ending of the mechanical unit and body overhaul work occurred when London Transport encountered problems of its own; as an expedient, London Country developed its own engine overhaul section at Guildford. But this was still insufficient to meet demand owing to the difficulty in obtaining spares and in particular for the (by now) 400 ex-London Transport buses dating from the early 1950s. Engine units were also sent to outside contractors for maintenance work.

A former Southdown Queen Mary-style Leyland Titan PD3 stands at West Croydon bus station on a 409 to Lingfield in May 1976.
Barry Le Jeune

So began a process of hiring vehicles in from elsewhere, or outright purchase. Hirers, with vehicle numbers in brackets, included Bournemouth Corporation (10), Eastbourne Borough Council (three), London Transport (variable), Maidstone Borough Council (six), Southend Transport (10), and Western National (six). The longest hires were those of five Bournemouth Atlanteans which were sent to Leatherhead, where they were employed from November 1975 to March 1978.

Secondhand purchases during the 1970s included 68 buses and coaches from Barton, Hants & Dorset, London Transport, Maidstone & District, Ribble and South Wales Transport. The same approach in the run-up to privatisation later brought 54 more Leyland Atlanteans to the company, from Southdown, Strathclyde and Northern Counties. Some vehicles were used for training duties rather than traffic, but the whole involved considerable movements of the fleet between garages. The result was that older vehicles were having to undergo recertification to keep them in service, while others were delicensed and robbed of any useful parts for use on those that could be kept going.

The commissioning of the Central Repair Works at Crawley in January 1976 saw the situation begin to improve again, and not before time, too. By September 1976, the number of delicensed vehicles was down to 65. Crawley dealt with mechanical work, body repairs and spray painting, also acting as a central stores.

Above: Reigate garage has a good selection of vehicles in this internal view showing, from left to right, Leyland National, Routemasters (two), MB, RT, LN, MB, LN and an RP. It is 1980. *John Glover*

Right: A garage plate (for Dorking), and alongside the duty number (4). *John Glover*

It was however not only keeping the fleets at work which was causing trouble. These were the years of chronic staff shortages; even if you had the buses, could you find the staff to crew them — given that this meant both driver and conductor in most instances? It might also be said that this was not a propitious situation for labour relations, given also the company's overwhelming financial need to cut operating costs if at all possible.

VEHICLE REQUIREMENTS

What vehicles were required to run the services? The summary of scheduled vehicles needed as of 15 May 1976 gives the answers.

Vehicle requirements, as at 15 May 1976

Type	Seats	Mon-Fri	Saturday	Sunday
RF	35-39	18	16	9
FT	16	3	3	-
BL	35	21	21	1
BN	35	25	21	7
RC	47	10	8	-
MB	45	25	22	13
MBS	33	68	58	13
SM	38/41	123	82	26
SMW	48/53	14	11	6
MS	45	6	4	3
LN	46	19	15	3
LNB	49	28	24	9
SNB	41	64	45	18
RP	45	6	3	1
Single-deck total		430	333	109

Type	Seats	Mon-Fri	Saturday	Sunday
RP	45	64	64	57
SMA	45	17	16	9
LNC	49	14	13	6
SNC	39	71	67	68
P	41/49	7	7	7
Coach total		173	167	147

	Mon-Fri	Saturday	Sunday
Double-deck total	331	242	59

	Mon-Fri	Saturday	Sunday
Fleet total	934	742	315

Note: includes the few traffic spares, staff bus and tours. Unfortunately the breakdown of double-deck buses by type is not available.

THE OPERATING ENVIRONMENT

Common to bus companies countrywide, the operating environment of these years was far from welcoming. As early as its first Annual Report in 1969, the NBC was moved to comment:

> 'In all too many cases, traffic management is interpreted as the introduction of one way systems in which traffic moves more quickly. In the process, the bus services are made much less accessible to passengers owing to the remoteness of the bus stops from which they wanted to start and finish.'

Traffic congestion and unrestricted parking were an impediment to bus movements in many towns.

This was expanded later with some concrete examples affecting London Country. The frequency, duration and location of delays to timetabled services attributable to traffic congestion was due to three main factors. With particular reference to Green Line, but relevant to bus services as well, these were:

- The volumes of peak movement to London
- The control of peak movements in suburban areas
- The control of off-peak flows.

Examples were given for each.

In June 1979, Green Line tests between Windsor and central London showed a normal journey time of 102-106 minutes, but peak journeys averaged 122-139 minutes. The principal causes were bottlenecks at the entrance to the central area. Hammersmith, Knightsbridge and Putney were among those mentioned, where traffic management measures were sufficient only to cope with average off-peak demand.

The build-up in suburban peaks was variable, depending on the degree to which commuting traffic combined with local works traffic or school journeys. These were often not individually long delays, but their cumulative effect was considerable. Thus, a test between Sidcup and Croydon in February 1981 showed traffic delays approaching traffic lights or roundabouts at Chislehurst (2min), Beckenham (3min), Elmers End (5min), Addiscombe (5min), East Croydon (6min), a total delay of 21 minutes on services operating a 15min headway. This was the equivalent of losing one complete bus, with one and a quarter miles still to go before reaching the terminus.

The primary cause was seen as the inadequacy of standard intersections to maintain flow with the volume of traffic at peak times. This could recur throughout the operating day. Thus Saturday shopping peaks at places like Croydon and Kingston created wide gaps in services which were attempting to offer a regular inter-urban frequency. It was the combination of these problems that was the main cause of the decision to terminate radial Green Line routes in central London, to make up time, at the expense of the loss of the cross-London services.

Off-peak delays are more unpredictable, with the result that the casual passenger was discouraged from future usage if timekeeping was disrupted by more than a few minutes. The Windsor-London express via the M4 was tested in June 1979. This service had a schedule time of 54 minutes. The actual off-peak time was 87 minutes. It was found that journeys on this route could average 48 to 62 minutes, but unexpected variations depended on the degree of congestion between Hammersmith and Victoria.

Left: An advertisement for the Harlow Pick-Me-Up service, a mixture of hail-&-ride and pre-booking using 16-seat Ford Transit minibuses. *Guy Brigden collection*

Right: If the ticket machine fails, what happens? The traditional answer was a stock of paper tickets of Edmondson size and progressively numbered, each with a pre-printed value. These were issued to the passenger in whatever combination of values to make up the fare paid. Sales revenue thus should be the sum of the value of all the tickets, confirmed by the numbers on those remaining. The ticket should be marked to indicate the number of the fare stage boarded. *Author's collection*

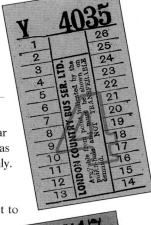

While the average time taken accorded with the scheduled time allocated, it was clear that faster running times and greater regularity could be achieved if a clearer run was possible, but also that unpredictable delays of up to half an hour could occur suddenly.

OPERATOR COSTS

It was the unpredictability of traffic congestion which was the greatest penalty cost to operators. If dislocation of the services was restricted to peak times, the additional cost to preserve a measure of reliability in each cast could be contained at one extra vehicle and an additional driver working only at peak times. If dislocation occurs throughout the day, this vehicle also requires to be manned throughout the working day for six days per week. The extra manning costs (the largest single factor of operating expenditure) are thus extended to more than 70 hours a week instead of 30 hours. In other words, two more drivers are needed instead of one.

The following is an actual example for the 707/717 London-Luton service. Originally four vehicles were used on high-efficiency duties, which earned route revenue covering their full costs, but the route later needed relief. The effect of peak augmentation was an additional 9% on weekly staff costs, plus one extra vehicle cost bringing the total vehicles to five (+25%). For further augmentation to cope with all day traffic dislocation, the additional staff costs rose to 17%, and the vehicle costs remained at an extra 25%. However, the increased revenue from improved reliability could meet only part of the additional cost. Over the whole route, approximately £70,000 (1980 prices) extra revenue or support from local authorities was needed to break even with the measures to improve service reliability.

Even with reliability issues tackled, the journey times were still expanding. This wasn't exactly a positive sales point, either. The same types of arguments can be applied to local bus services.

CREWING

If there was one single policy matter that London Country needed to attend to quickly, it was the crewing of buses and getting the costs down. That meant the conversion to one-man operation in the jargon of the day, but this was unlikely to be popular with the platform staff. It could proceed only as fast as the fleet replacement programme would allow.

The following is the text of an address to the staff on the subject by the then Managing Director, C. R. Buckley:

'The single manning of buses on services of the urban and rural types of operation provided by London Country is a natural development as the number of passengers continues to decrease. The management and trade unions are continually examining ticket and money box systems to make the job of one man operation as easy and efficient as possible. There is no doubt that the Stevenage Superbus concept will be extended for use elsewhere and we aim to win back passengers from the ever increasing number of private cars with more reliable and quicker services.'

The message seemed to be that the complex fares systems were likely to be replaced, though in the event the maximising of revenue wherever possible became the guiding light.

STEVENAGE SUPERBUS

The New Towns were always keen to see new services implemented. In Stevenage, the Development Corporation's public transport scheme comprised express bus services routed along the primary roads from termini in the residential areas, serving the industrial area with a five-minute frequency at peak times and terminating at the town centre. Superbus services were inaugurated in 1971 and 1972,

following an earlier experiment with a special peak-period service with pre-booked seats superimposed on the existing timetable.

Superbus certainly had its successes, through providing a regular, frequent, reliable and relatively fast flat-fare service with limited stops. When it began in May 1971, there were 17,300 passenger journeys a week on the Chells Superbus, representing 4.3 trips per household; a year later there were more than 42,000. Numbers continued to grow, albeit not so spectacularly. The weekly deficit was £738 per week. However, the modal split of workers to the town centre or the industrial estate by car dropped from 66% to 46% over the first three years.

Superbus was under the auspices of the Department of the Environment, which was investigating the provision of intensive bus services as an alternative to extra expenditure on roads. London Country used the Metro-Scanias.

HARLOW PICK-ME-UP

The Harlow Pick-Me-Up bus was an early project which came to fruition in 1974, using the five Ford Transits with Dormobile bodywork. This account is abridged from London Country's explanatory booklet:

'The Pick-Me-Up-Bus is a new idea in public transport, specially applied to give residents in Old Harlow the most practical type of Bus link with the town centre and other points such as Harlow Town station, the Princess Alexandra Hospital, and within Old Harlow itself.

'The Pick-Me-Up-Bus provides a service with a difference. It will actually collect you straight from your home or a nearby street corner, and will later bring you back. You, the passenger, decide the time you want the bus to fetch you. All this at a single fare of only 10p, children 8p, old age pensioners 5p.'

How pick-me-up works
'Each of the sixteen-seater Pick-Me-Up buses is radio-controlled from an office at the Bus Station. When you want to be collected (and there are only a few roads where the buses cannot go), contact the Despatcher and tell him your requirements. He will make the booking and tell you when to expect the bus.

'Ring him on Harlow 39993 or use one of the 11 Pick-Me-Up Freephones on the streets. If you need to catch a train or keep an appointment, tell the Despatcher. Usually he will be able to have the Pick-Me-

Left: LNB46 is hoisted for attention in the Central Repair Works at Crawley on 13 July 1980. *Guy Brigden*

Above: The new NBC bus livery. RF278, the first RF to carry this livery, was totally devoid of lining or other relief other than the company name. It looked worse when it was dirty. *London Country*

Up Bus at your door within 30 minutes. But he will need at least 45 minutes notice in order to do so with absolute certainty.

'Reply paid postcards can also be used, using the post or the special box on the bus. However, you must leave time for confirmation of your booking to be sent to you.'

Operation

'The buses operate between 07.00 and 23.00 Mondays to Saturdays. Besides providing the bookable door-to-door service, they can be stopped and boarded anywhere in Old Harlow. There is no fixed timetable, but the map (provided) will show you the roads they must always take. If you wait on any of these, a bus should be along within 20 mins up to 19.00, hourly after that.

'In the town centre, a bus leaves the bus station approximately every 20mins and you can see from the clock outside the Pick-Me-Up office when the next departure is due. Just board the waiting bus and tell the driver where you want to go in Old Harlow. Remember, pre-booked passengers will have priority.

'Between 16.55 and 19.00 buses always call at Harlow Town station to meet trains from London. At other times you must call the Despatcher to be picked up, or at any time from the Hospital. In the evenings, the route is extended to serve the Playhouse, Cinema and Bingo.'

After booking

'After you have made your booking, please be ready when the Bus arrives, as it cannot wait beyond the pick up time you have been given. Also have your exact fare ready before boarding, then drop it into the farebox by the driver and take your seat quickly, leaving the entrance clear for other passengers. A quick get away is important to keep the service running on time.'

The experimental service was sponsored by the Department of the Environment, Harlow District Council, Harlow Development Corporation and Essex County Council, with the service operated by London Country Bus Services Ltd. Its problems, as would later be demonstrated elsewhere, centred on the extra cost of maintaining a control office and the booking procedures, when compared with an ordinary timetabled operation. The service was discontinued in 1977, to be replaced by a conventional operation using BNs instead of the Transits.

INFLATION

In the latter 1960s, the Retail Price Index began to rise, and by the beginning of 1969 had reached an annual rate of over 6%. Some respite followed, only to peak in summer 1971 at 10.3%. Again the RPI fell back to a low point of 5.8% in July 1972, but it then really started to climb. 1974 started at 12.0%, and a year later it was 19.9%. The highest point reached was an annual rate of increases in retail prices of 26.9% in September 1975. Rates then fell slowly, but it was April the following year before it was below 20% and 1978 until it was less than 10%. In 1979 to 1982 there was a repeat performance, but the peak this time was a mere 21.9%, reached in May 1980.

The creation of London Country Bus Services in 1970 exposed the company to the worst of all this. Having been subject to varying degrees of price restraint in the previous decade as part of London Transport, it became necessary to increase income as quickly as it could. Fares increases to match inflation at these sorts of rates were unavoidable, but these also had to take into account what the industry terms 'recession', the loss of patronage that results. Given a price increase of (say) 10% gross, the yield will be less as a proportion of those affected will decide not to travel. How many will so decide is something for the informed guessing department, but it is a factor that needs to be taken into account.

If there is also an underlying downward trend of patronage, that is another factor. The company can try and match this by a proportionate reduction in operating costs, but this is very difficult given the incidence of all the various overheads etc. The risk is that of losing more patronage and hence fares income than is saved in cost reductions.

As a result, future financial outcomes become very difficult to predict. If a company needs revenue support on what turned out to be a quite large scale, as London Country did, this is the outcome of the interaction between costs and revenues. These are not directly related, and unforeseen events in the case of either can have a disproportionate result on the outcome.

Bus operations are labour intensive, and 70% of all LCBS expenditure was on payroll. The effects of inflation were colossal, and this alone was enough to require major fare increases in quick succession. Until 1980, fares had to be the subject of formal applications made to the Traffic Commissioner, who would hold a public hearing where any formal objections were made. The adult single fares for distances of one, two and three miles are shown below:

Adult single fares in pence, London Country Bus Services

Effective date	Distance		
	1 mile	2 miles	3 miles
1 January 1970	2.5p	4p	5p
19 August 1974	7p	9p	11p
23 March 1975	8p	11p	14p
13 July 1975	9p	12p	14p
19 October 1975	10p	14p	18p
11 April 1976	11p	15p	20p
1 January 1977	12p	17p	22p
25 October 1977	14p	20p	26p
1 April 1978	15p	23p	30p
31 March 1979	16p	26p	33p
9 September 1979	17p	28p	36p
29 March 1980	20p	33p	42p
8 March 1981	22p	37p	48p
4 October 1981	23p	38p	49p
21 March 1982	25p	42p	54p
27 March 1983	27p	45p	58p

Above: The Harlow Pick-Me-Up Ford Transit minibuses carried no route number. This is FT3. *Ford Motor Co*

Apart from the unrecorded period between 1970 and 1974, this is thought to be a complete list of the fares increases made by the company. In the ten years to 1980, fares rose by a factor of about eight. After 1980, fares were no longer controlled and were tailored more to individual counties. Thus they do not necessarily apply to the operation as a whole.

CHILD FARES

Early commercial action by London Country saw child fares rise as a proportion of adult fares from half fare to three quarters. This was followed by a further adjustment to a fare which was applicable to adults off-peak (1p less than the adult peak fare) and children at peak. March 1975 saw this curious mixture abandoned, much to the relief no doubt of bus crews who had to handle it, to be replaced by a standard adult single fare at all times, also payable by children at specified peak hours. The three quarters fare for children remained off-peak, though this was soon dropped to half fare at all off-peak times. The end of the peak was also pulled back from 19.00 to 18.30. Throughout, it should be remembered that children were defined as under 14; those of 14 and over were charged as adults.

Such charging policies, understandable as they may have been from an economic standpoint, still caused huge public resentment. Child fares were restored to half fare at all times from 31 March 1979 in Hertfordshire and on 29 March 1980 in Surrey; in both cases the County Councils agreed to make compensatory payments. The change in age limits so that child fares applied to all those aged 5 and under 16 had to wait until 1983.

Day return fares were available, normally at the end of the morning peak and all day at weekends.

Other fares, this time with a major local authority input, were concessions for the elderly. Here, schemes

Above right: The Bournemouth Fleetlines were on hire to London Country longer than any other vehicle. Leatherhead-based, this was No 194 on the 408 from Croydon to Guildford, on the short section of the Ewell bypass used by this route on 14 May 1976. *Guy Brigden*

Right: This Maidstone Borough Council Massey-bodied Leyland Atlantean, No 39, is outside Chelsham Garage on a 403 to Warlingham Park Hospital. *Ian Allan Library*

Below: The first SMA to be received by London Country, SMA1, very smartly turned out for photographic purposes with the blind display just in the right position and the driver wearing a full uniform. The 'Flying Polo' logo is very apparent. *Ian Allan Library*

which involved London Transport and London Country had to be reconstituted, the most usual outcome being a uniform concession which was available on any bus throughout the County concerned (with time restrictions), but issued and financed by the District Councils.

THE FINANCIAL PICTURE

The table shows the outcome for London Country for the calendar (and not local authority financial) years 1976-1983. The major problems of financial shortfalls at the beginning of the period and not shown here were beginning to recede, but it was some time before the situation could really be said to be under control. As can be seen, the borrowing from the National Bus Company which was required resulted in considerable interest payments. Unfortunately, earlier years were not included in this analysis.

Revenue support, it will be noted, never reached the level where it accounted for as much as 20% of the company's income, though it came close in 1980 (19%).

London Country Bus Services Ltd Financial statistics 1976-1983 at out-turn prices

Year	Revenue	Expenditure	Deficit	Revenue support	Loss/profit	Borrowing	Interest charge
	£'000	£'000	£'000	£'000	£'000	£'000	£'000
1976	21,311	28,043	6,732	3,228	-3,504	8,643	915
1977	22,578	29,757	7,179	4,067	-3,112	12,230	1,277
1978	25,610	31,130	5,520	4,640	-880	11,773	1,400
1979	28,255	34,566	6,311	6,561	250	11,400	1,345
					(1)		
1980	32,682	40,382	7,700	7,404	-296	9,956	1,220
1981	35,877	43,216	7,339	7,561	222	6,824	921
					(2)		
1982	40,456	49,147	8,691	9,909	1,218	3,429	468
					(3)		
1983	44,313	53,015	8,702	9,124	422	4,527	348
					(4)		

Notes: (1) Includes profit of £171,000 on sale of assets. (2) Includes profit of £112,000 on sale of assets. (3) Includes net profit on unsupported network and miscellaneous activities £699,000 and Transport Supplementary Grant in respect of previous years £519,000. (4) Includes profit on sale of assets.

Source: LCBS paper to Hertfordshire County Council, 5 December 1984

NBC

And how were relations with the parent company, NBC? Viewed from the outside, these always seemed to be a little fraught. LCBS quite clearly was far from the normal mould in terms of a standard NBC subsidiary. When an NBC management restructuring divided the local bus operating companies into three regions (Eastern, Southern and Western), LCBS remained a separate entity within the Southern region.

In 1975/76, senior NBC managers gave evidence to the House of Commons Select Committee on Nationalised Industries, in which they said that the National Bus Company had been *compelled* to absorb LCBS (author's italics). Well, maybe, but it is all part of the job and doesn't make for a happy ship.

Later, NBC developed the Market Analysis Project (MAP). Trialled in a number of areas, it was later rolled out nationwide. The aim was to identify systematically, by areas, bus service networks which could be maintained in the long term at commercially acceptable fares levels. It would also bring to light the situations or routes in which revenue support would be needed to continue bus service provision. Attention could then be directed to social needs and how they could be met. This was to be carried out by the NBC subsidiaries, largely independent of any County Council input or views.

London Country, while appreciating what was being done, preferred to continue its close liaison with the

London Country had relatively few Daimler Fleetlines of its own; this is AF4, with no garage allocation, but with displays for the 410 to Biggin Hill. *NBC/Ian Allan Library*

County Councils in its area and develop schemes jointly. It was with considerable satisfaction that the large scheme developed for the Croydon-Guildford corridor and implemented in 1980 (see later) was found to give considerably better results than the MAP scheme introduced at the same time in west Surrey.

The Government's Transport Policy White Paper of 1976 canvassed the ideal of reorganising the operating boundaries of NBC companies to accord more closely with those of County Councils, but nothing came of it.

MARKETING

Although always properly known as London Country, the expansion of bus networks in the more urban parts of the operation sometimes gave the opportunity to create a new marketing identity. Of particular note was where bus networks were redesigned from scratch, following extensive survey work and in close co-operation with the County and District Councils. These were given names aimed at building up a local affinity, as follows:

Watford and Rickmansworth, Herts	Watfordwide
Stevenage, Herts	Stevenage Bus
Crawley, West Sussex	C-Line
Harlow, Essex	Townbus

Similar town networks, with routes linked by a common prefix letter (eg S4, H15, G3), although having no specific marketing name, were introduced in St Albans, Hemel Hempstead and Guildford, the last in conjunction with three other operators. In each case, 'Travelwide' season tickets were introduced to allow unlimited travel in the local area, and free maps and timetables were distributed door-to-door to encourage bus use.

Similar techniques were employed in rural areas on the western side of London Country's operation, as part of the MAP reorganisation carried out by NBC company Alder Valley and jointly operated with them. These were in High Wycombe, Amersham and Chesham (Chilternlink), Slough and Windsor (Thameslink) and Guildford, Woking and Chertsey (Weyfarer).

C-LINE

C-Line was probably London Country's biggest-ever service reorganisation in one location, which began on 1 July 1978. The 10 Crawley town services were replaced by eight routes, C1-C8, which also covered the newly developed residential areas for the first time and gave other existing estates their first Sunday service. Three further peak routes, C15-C17, were designed to give fast connections between residential areas and the industrial zone, and there was a schools special, C21.

A fleet of 24 new Atlanteans fitted with fareboxes were used to launch the service and a flat fare, initially 20p, was charged. This overcame the anomalies inherent with a system of distance-related fares and routes which perform loops around the estates; inevitably there comes a point where, rather than wait any longer, it is quicker to catch the next bus which happens to be on the other side of the road but has further to travel — so the fare is more.

A Crawleywide weekly or monthly ticket was also introduced.

TIMETABLES

The potential for similar schemes elsewhere was felt to be limited by the low density of many parts of the network in the more rural areas. To encourage traffic on these, the company timetables, which were in a pocket-sized form largely inherited from London Transport, were redesigned. The new versions were A5 and made extensive use of colour, with a monochrome drawing on the cover showing some local feature. They included the services of all operators, not just London Country, and a comprehensive route map. This was supported where necessary by individual town maps to show precise routeings and street names. The whole was comprehensively indexed and there was a diagram of the local rail services. In many ways, they were a model of their type.

Appearing progressively from 1979 onwards, the series of 11 publications covered the following areas:

1　Green Line
2　Gravesend, Dartford and Swanley
3　Sevenoaks
4　Crawley and East Grinstead
5　East Surrey
6　Guildford and Woking
7　Slough and Windsor
8　South Buckinghamshire
9　West Hertfordshire
10　Central Hertfordshire
11　Harlow and Hertford

The original list was later modified and latterly 16 books were produced. As time went on, the areas covered became smaller. Thus East Surrey gave way to Epsom and Leatherhead, Dorking and Reigate, and Tandridge. It is uncertain whether all the books which at one time or another were listed ever appeared. Many extended to three or so successive editions.

However, a more austere regime set in after 1984 in the run-up to deregulation, of which more later; the books were renamed 'Travellers Times' and were advertised as being 'YourLondonCountryBusandGreenLineCoachGuide', all of which apparently formed one word! The services of other operators might or might not appear.

One-man buses

Many London Country bus routes are one-man operated so that they can be run more economically, with fewer but better paid staff.

So please have your exact fare ready to pay as you board—it will save you time

An advertisement which appeared in many forms, in this case inside a 1974 timetable. One of the biggest problems with one-man operation is boarding time which can have severe repercussions on the end-to-end running time. This was at least an attempt to try and speed things up. *London Country*

4

Rural
Bus Grant

*'Many (bus) companies are too sure that they know what best suits
their own and the public interest.'*

David St John Thomas, 1963

The 1968 Transport Act took the opportunity to give local authorities powers in relation to local bus services, which was a new departure. Section 34(1) of the Act reads:

'Any of the following councils, namely the council of any county, county borough or county district in England... or any two or more of those councils acting jointly, may, on such conditions, if any, they think fit, afford assistance... by way of grant, loan or both, for the purposes of securing the provision, improvement or continuance of any bus or ferry service if in the opinion of the council... that service is or will be for the benefit of persons residing in rural areas.'

The Minister was prepared to meet half the cost of the sums thus committed.

Well, it was a start, though the powers were far from clear-cut in terms of who in local authority terms was expected to exercise them (and thus a likely source of dispute) and the interpretation of 'rural', which the Act did not attempt to define. Nor did it cover services for people in towns visiting the countryside.

As it turned out, the advent of the rural bus grant was a portent for what was to become a far wider commitment for County Councils in the future. The powers contained in this Act were in all senses discretionary; it was up to the Councils concerned as to whether or not they wished to exercise them and, if so, to what extent.

Few authorities by that stage could have been completely unaware of the plight of rural buses, but knowledge of what useful services they were performing for the public was scanty. If it came to the point of withdrawal, were they worth retaining? There was still, in essence, a feeling that commercial services should live or die in terms of their ability to make a profit for their owners. But the experience of recent years had demonstrated continuous cutbacks in services, and though this was not a matter that was a responsibility of the elected Members, they nevertheless were aware of the fears of their constituents.

Everything was put into sharper focus when what might be described as 'demands with menaces' arrived from Reigate on County Council doorsteps in October 1970. 'Dear Sir,' it began, 'The recent and continuing deterioration of the financial position of London Country Bus Services Ltd makes it essential to take urgent steps...' The rest can be imagined. It is one thing to be aware of a problem, but another matter altogether to get a bill for sorting it out!

REACTIONS

An early decision to be made was whether this was a matter to be dealt with by County Councils, District Councils, or both. London Country was in a hurry; three months was, in its view, sufficient time for local authorities to make up their minds, at least in principle, whether or not to give any assistance. It later became clear that the company would be prepared to continue operation if a starting date for some permanent arrangement could be fixed and an interim arrangement made until then. On the other hand, no agreement and the service would cease.

On a damp day, RF550 works a 331 to Standon from Hertford bus station. What might, or might not, constitute a rural bus service is open to some doubt, but this one was definitely included. *Barry Le Jeune*

As collated by London Country, the following arrangements had been made, on a county-by-county basis, by mid-April 1971. The UDCs and RDCs referred to were Urban and Rural District Councils respectively.

Bedfordshire

'The local Councils appear not to be getting any advice or direction from the County Council. A declaration of intent was requested by the end of February.

'We have been verbally informed that the Luton and Dunstable Councils have been urged to take decisions on the services operating in their areas, and if bus grants are agreed upon the County Council will assist in the coordination with other authorities.

'No official reply has been received from the County Council, but again it is understood that assistance will be given where required. There appears to be considerable dissension amongst local councils on this point and finality has not yet been reached.

'A similar decision to that of Buckinghamshire (no direct grants) has now been received from Bedfordshire.

'Luton and Dunstable RDCs have now decided not to participate in the provision of bus grants. Invitations have now been sent to all local Authorities concerned to attend a meeting in an endeavour to reach finality, particularly in respect of routes which Hertfordshire wish to support but with which local agreement has failed up to now.'

Buckinghamshire

'The County Council have still made no move to coordinate the efforts of local Councils, in fact, one RDC has announced in the Press its agreement to provide bus grants and two other Councils have informed us by telephone of their intention also to support. This lack of leadership has led to much anxiety amongst the travelling public and unfair criticism of the company at local Council meetings.

BN66, a Bristol LH in a garage, possibly Amersham. These were the new models for rural services to replace the ageing RFs, though their lifespan turned out to be many years shorter. Although the livery looks like standard NBC, a 'North West' symbol replaces the NBC symbol, showing this is soon after the division of London Country into four. *Author's collection*

'A declaration of intent was requested by the end of February. No official reply was received from the County Council, who, we understand, are agreeable to assist any Local Authority who indicates its desire to provide bus grants.

'The County Council have now officially stated that they will not make any bus grants direct, but will contribute equally with Local Authorities to make up the deficit after the Minister's grant of 50% for any service which is required to be continued.

'The County Treasurer has undertaken to coordinate for the local authorities. Meantime, we have obtained promises for bus grants from Eton RDC for six months and Chesham RDC for three months.

'The promised coordination now appears to concern only the apportionment of the deficit between the various Local Authorities, the latter still have to negotiate separately with the company. Meetings have taken place with Amersham & Chesham UDC, from which it is hoped agreement will be reached.'

East Sussex
'A further reminder has been sent to the Council, asking them for a declaration of intent. The Council referred route 494 to the East Grinstead UDC in whose area it operated, but have mentioned that it is unlikely that a bus grant will be forthcoming. We have advised the County Council to make attempts to convince the UDC to support Surrey County Council in grant aiding this service. The upshot was that East Sussex did not agree to provide a bus for their section of the one route under review.'

Essex
'We have met the County Council on the financial details and they appear to be agreeable to fall in with Hertfordshire where routes overlap. A meeting has taken place with the local Councils at which the

County Council was present. All the routes affecting Essex are joint with Hertfordshire, whose decision is awaited before Essex commit themselves. They appear, however, not to be averse to bus grants.

'Official decision now received that Essex will be providing bus grants on the same conditions as Hertfordshire on common routes. Agreed to pay grants for 20 services for a period of six months in two instalments.'

Hertfordshire

'Officers of the Treasurer's department met LCBS. Meetings of groups of Local Authorities took place to discuss traffic needs, but the County Council have not yet agreed to participate or given any lead in coordinating the efforts of the groups. Berkhamsted RDC indicated their support as has Hitchin RDC, and the County Council have been asked for a general declaration of intent. There is every indication that the council will participate in the promotion of grants for certain services.

'In a complete turnaround of attitude, the County Council agreed to provide In full grants for all services required by Local Authorities to be continued for a period of six months. Thereafter, the local councils must decide which services they need to be preserved and the County Council will pay half the bus grants needed to ensure the continuance of these routes. The County Council officers have been met and it seems that grants will be forthcoming for the majority of services apart from certain cases where the qualification for Ministry grant is in some doubt.

'Discussions continued towards finality. Problems arose with routes running into Buckinghamshire and Bedfordshire, where some local authorities were unwilling to support bus grants. Hertfordshire agreed to pay bus grants for twenty services for a period of six months, in two instalments.'

Kent

'The County Council are prepared to make bus grants for a limited period. LCBS have now met an Officer of the Treasurer's department to explain the financial statistics. The London Borough of Bromley appear to be interested in participation as far as the section of route 410 between Biggin Hill and Bromley is concerned, later confirmed by Bromley. Draft conditions of agreements received and meeting arranged to discuss amendments to services. Kent agreed to pay bus grants for all services under review for a period of twelve months in quarterly instalments.'

Surrey

'The County Council issued a press notice indicating the position to date and this has done much to allay the fears of the people. There have been meetings with Officers to discuss financial details. The County Council commenced a study of all transport facilities in the area, and a first meeting has been held with this team. The Council have agreed to pay bus grants for all services under review for a period of twelve months, in quarterly instalments.'

West Sussex

'We learn that the County Council are prepared to support a bus grant. They hope to leave the negotiations for payment of a bus grant for 426 to Surrey, who are also concerned with this route. Draft conditions of agreement received, and agreement to provide a bus grant for the small section of one route under review for a period of twelve months. Payments to be made by four equal instalments.'

The file contents end at this point, though there is enough to be able to discern the underlying attitudes, many of which were to be reinforced in the years to come. The boundary problem was clearly a major issue, both in practical terms and financially. Another issue was the responsibilities of the various levels of local government. How well was the whole issue understood at that time, anyway? Again, it was to emerge that much was still to be learned, by just about everyone.

One of those matters was the propensity of authorities to object before the Traffic Commissioners to operator proposals for fare increases.

Rural grants in Hertfordshire?

The services listed as requiring rural bus grant in Hertfordshire were in substantial numbers, and the end of 1970 brought a long list:

304	COLNEY STREET, Wheathampstead, HITCHIN
308	HERTFORD, Bayford, GOFFS OAK
309/A	NORTHWOOD, Rickmansworth, CHORLEYWOOD
317/A	HEMEL HEMPSTEAD STATION, Great Gaddesden, BERKHAMSTED
317A	TWO WATERS, Hemel Hempstead, Little Gaddesden, BERKHAMSTED
327	HERTFORD, Hoddesdon, NAZEING
329	HERTFORD, Knebworth, NUP END
331/A	HERTFORD, Standon, BUNTINGFORD
335	WATFORD, Chalfont St Giles, Slough, WINDSOR
336/A	WATFORD, Rickmansworth, Amersham, CHESHAM
337	DUNSTABLE, HEMEL HEMPSTEAD STATION
350/A	NEW BARNET STATION, Hertford, BISHOP'S STORTFORD
351	BUNTINGFORD, WARE, MUCH HADHAM (Limited Stop Service)
364/A	FLAMSTEAD VILLAGE, Luton, HITCHIN
381	EASTWICK, Epping, TOOT HILL or COOPERSALE COMMON
382	ST ALBANS, Welwyn, CODICOTE
384/A	LETCHWORTH, Stevenage, Ware, HERTFORD
386	BISHOP'S STORTFORD, Buntingford, HITCHIN
388	HARLOW, Ware, MARDLEY HILL or WELWYN GARDEN CITY
390	SAWBRIDGEWORTH, St Margarets, STEVENAGE
393/A	WELWYN GARDEN CITY, Hertford, HARLOW
807	LETCHWORTH, Weston, STEVENAGE

It was thus a far from marginal exercise as far as London Country was concerned; together these buses were covering about 2.8million miles a year.

Non-rural services

It was still only the rural services for which London Country (like any bus company anywhere at that time) was able to make claims. The other services were undergoing a continuous programme of modification and reassessment from the birth of the company in 1970 and which in the event continued for many years.

In general, cross-subsidy between routes was to be discouraged and minimised. All parts of the operation were affected, and rural services which Councils decided they did not wish to keep were withdrawn.

Again, it is not practicable to do more than give some examples of what these changes meant:

- The 329, 351, 381 and 807 were to receive no financial support and were withdrawn on 7 August 1971
- The Monday-Friday journeys on the 321 were reduced between Harpenden and Uxbridge in the morning peak and generally halved at other times, same date
- The 704/705/715/715A group of Green Line services all ceased double-deck crew operation and were converted to RP coaches, March 1972. The 706 frequency was reduced
- The 724 Green Line was withdrawn between Rickmansworth and High Wycombe, and rerouted to Heathrow Airport and Staines, 20 May 1972
- The 410 was converted from crewed double-deck operation to new Fleetline omo operation on 19 December 1972

XF5, a Daimler Fleetline on the 424 to East Grinstead. The 424 had the incidence of a heavy schools commitment, which was not helpful for its economics. It was mainly for this reason that double-deckers remained on this essentially rural route. *Author's collection*

- Buses 804/A/B were converted from MBS single-deck (bus capacity 60) to double-deck omo using new Atlanteans (72 seats). Mileage-based fares were replaced by 6p flat fares for adults, 5p for children, issued by drivers using Farebox, no change given (and no Rovers issued). This took effect from 9 September 1972.

Concurrently, fares conditions were revised, particularly in relation to children. In August 1970 Scholars' Identity Cards to enable children aged 14-18 to travel at child fares were charged at 65p per card, based on 1p for each of 190 days of school in a year, divided by three to give a termly rate. Peak charging was also introduced.

SURREY'S APPROACH

What was to be done? Surrey County Council decided that in the short term they would meet the requests for payment, but that this would be followed up with a detailed examination on a route-by-route basis.

An early exercise was to draw up a list of questions and answers for the actual decision on whether a particular route should be subsidised, or allowed to vanish. What actually transpired was that all routes examined showed either that the cost per passenger would be astronomical, or quite modest, which made the decision relatively easy.

Cards were distributed on buses and every passenger was asked to complete them with details of their journey and so on. The reason for the survey was explained and that completion of the card might help retain the route. Completion rates approached 100%! It was decided in a few cases that the subsidy requested was so low, there was little point in carrying out a route survey as the cost would exceed the subsidy.

The next step was to draw up criteria for route assessment. Where a route is provided for the benefit of the rural population, what exactly is meant? It consists of various objectives that the population wishes to achieve. These range from journeys necessary for continuing a rural way of life to journeys which fulfil the occasional desire to travel to a particular place for pleasure.

It was decided there were four objectives. Those to education or to work (or on business) were the top requirements and both were deemed essential, followed by shopping (desirable) and all other journeys at a lower level.

Standard means of assessment were then drawn up of the cost to people in each of the four categories should the service be withdrawn. With education journeys, this meant a means of calculating the cost of extra school buses based on an average cost per mile, after a check that existing services in the area with spare capacity couldn't be used. Business and work journeys were measured, using, in the case of taxis and cars, an occupancy rate similar to that found in other similar studies. On shopping journeys, the possibility of a bus service on certain days of the week only was studied; this leaves the bus available to run similar journeys to other destinations on the other days. Other journeys, mainly pleasure trips by villagers to the towns or townspeople to the countryside, are difficult to assess, but it was decided to see the cost/benefit to the community of having the bus available for the other three types of trips, compare this with the subsidy and then decide whether the balance left was worth the required subsidy.

A brief look at interviewing people in their homes was enough: data collected in this way would be too costly, and difficult to organise if criteria such as boundaries of half-mile distance from bus routes to home were to be followed.

ON-BUS SURVEYS

Thus Surrey adopted the system of on-bus survey, and it proved most successful. Reply paid cards were handed out on the bus and on a census day every journey was covered by a surveyor who, in practice, and with skill, managed to persuade almost everyone to hand back completed cards before leaving the bus.

Organisation of the schedules for the survey teams was a real work of art, but it was because every bus journey was covered that a comprehensive and accurate picture could be built up. A graphical representation of each bus on the route was drawn up, and two shift schedules for the survey team, who had the choice of working just one shift or both. In any event, all buses were covered.

Route schedules were compiled, giving each bus stop (all were given a unique number), meal breaks and location of toilets. A County Council-owned caravan was found to make an ideal base, since it could be stationed at a remote or otherwise inconvenient spot, enabled the survey staff to have a break in comfort, make a cup of tea or have a hot snack. Members of the survey staff themselves were a mixture of housewives, retired people and others, most of whom were regular surveyors.

The surveys themselves were made on a weekday, often Thursday as this was not normally an early closing day in Surrey, and as required on Saturdays and Sundays. Coverage included quite busy double-deck routes, not necessarily loss making, but surveyed to build up a more comprehensive picture of the public transport scene. Such information also helped to pinpoint any spare capacity so that, for example, a small deviation by an odd journey or two off-route might enable a shopping service to be provided for the inhabitants of a small hamlet.

Extracts from all this were compiled into a small route précis sheet for each service (see example, below), which detailed route, operator, District Council areas covered, number of buses used, frequency, alternative services, survey days, total passengers, peak-hour traffic and the total traffic on the route carried at peak hours, major boarding points, main passenger movements (defined as common points between which more than 10 passengers were carried) and the journey purpose.

The information from these sheets was also used for two diagrams. One was a fairly simple one in graph form showing passenger totals per journey, with different colours for the subtotals for each journey purpose. The other, a more elaborate but most revealing diagram, showed total passenger journeys on a route for the

Above: RF682 heads back towards Dunstable from Dagnall on the last Wednesday of operation of the 352 route. It was operated subsequently by Court Line Coaches. *Ian Allan Library*

Below: Not really a rural route, but by 1980 the 472 was running one journey each way between Leatherhead and Netherne Hospital on Wednesday and Sunday afternoons only. It had a restricted service in that passengers on the inward journey were not allowed to alight anywhere except at the terminus, and that was also the only point at which they could board on the return journey. This is BN42 in Ewell on 23 April 1978 and the bus is not exactly overwhelmed with custom. *Guy Brigden*

The 462 linking Leatherhead with Staines was described as a rural inter-town route, whose usage had always been modest. It is operated here with a Green Line RF, passing through Addlestone. Progressive economies were to see its eventual demise. *Ian Allan Library*

day, by individual totals for each stop. The thickness of the lines on the diagram was proportional to the total number of journeys being made, in each direction, so that the chart was a veritable mine of information. It also helped demonstrate the essential characteristics of the travel patterns on the route.

Later, the survey programme was expanded to many more routes throughout Surrey, coupled perhaps with interview surveys. However, the main thrust changed on busy routes to head counting of the ons and offs at each stop, from which the total numbers on board the bus at any time could be ascertained. The graphical presentation gave way to large sheets of paper, on which successive vehicle journeys on each route could be seen, totalled and compared.

The methods used have been described in some detail, since the basic approach is still valid. Times move on, though, and today much can be derived from ticket machine data, though this will not provide journey purpose. The Surrey system described was operable long before ticket machines offered any data other than the money taken reconciled with the total number and value of the tickets issued. Thus return tickets presented to the driver would be cancelled, but not recorded anywhere. Ticket machines of those days were good for cash control, which was after all their main purpose, but precious little else.

This is the Route Précis sheet compiled for a group of three routes, which involved both Surrey and Kent County Councils:

Routes operated by London Country Bus Services Ltd

464   Staffhurst Wood-Holland-Hurst Green-Old Oxted-Oxted-Limpsfield-Chart-Crockham Hill-Froghole-Westerham. Additional journeys: Oxted-Titsey-Chelsham, Oxted-Titsey-Tatsfield, to Oxted, Gordons Way, through Pollards Oak Estate, Oxted.

465   Staffhurst Wood-Holland-Hurst Green-Old Oxted-Oxted-Limpsfield-Chart-Crockham Hill-Marlpit Hill-Edenbridge

485   Westerham-Froghole-Crockham Hill-Marlpit Hill-Edenbridge

Surrey sections
464/5 Staffhurst Wood-Kent Hatch (Chart)
485   Nil

Local authorities
    Godstone RDC, Surrey
    Kent County Council

Type of operation
    Single-deck RF-type buses, one-man operated from Chelsham Garage. The three routes are operated as follows:
464   Holland-Westerham
465   Westerham-Edenbridge
485   Edenbridge-Holland, and vice versa.
    No Sunday service.
    No of buses used   3

Service interval (mins)	Weekday		Saturday
	Peak	Off peak	
Crockham Hill-Edenbridge	60	30-90	30-90
Crockham Hill-Westerham	60	30-90	30-90
Holland-Chart	30	60	irregular
Oxted-Chelsham	irregular	irregular	irregular

Alternative services:

Old Oxted-Limpsfield	410
Old Oxted-Oxted	410, 494
Marlpit Hill-Edenbridge	434, M&D 135, 93
Oxted-Hurst Green-Edenbridge	train
Oxted-Westerham	410 (main road 410 service)

Survey date
Thursday 1 July 1971, Saturday 26 June 1971. All journeys covered.

Number of passengers

	Route	Total passengers	Of which, those with no alternatives
Thursday	464	591	563
	465	328	305
	485	130	105
Total		1,049	973
Saturday	464	293	271
	465	273	251
	485	85	79
Total		651	601

Peak hours
In the weekday peak periods (07.30-09.00 and 17.00-18.30), the following passengers were carried:

464	171	29% of the total
465	78	24% of the total
485	14	11% of the total

Major boarding points

464/5   Chart, Oxted Station East Side, Oxted Council Offices, Limpsfield Common Schools, Oxted Police Station, Holland Post Office, Holland Coldshott, Merle Common Primary School, Pollards Oak Crescent.

485   Westerham Green

Main movements (over 15 journeys)
Thursday

464/5	Holland Coldshott-Oxted Police Station	16
464	Merle Common School-Holland Post Office	31
464	Merle Common School-Holland Coldshott	34
464	Holland Post Office-Merle Common School	39
464	Pollards Oak Crescent-Limpsfield Common School	23
464	Limpsfield Common School-Pollards Oak Crescent	23
465	Holland Post Office-Merle Common School	25
485	Edenbridge Post Office-Westerham Green	15

Saturday

464	Oxted Station East-Chart	25
464	Holland Coldshott-Oxted Station East	16
465	Oxted Station East-Chart	23
465	Oxted Police Station-Holland Post Office	15
485	nil	

Journey purpose

	Thursday				Saturday			
	464	465	485	Total	464	465	485	Total
Work & business	124	83	36	243	54	41	11	106
Education	273	82	10	365	8	0	0	8
Shopping	128	101	47	276	150	142	27	319
Other	66	62	37	165	82	90	47	219
Total	591	328	130	1,049	294	273	85	652

Age groups

	464	465	485	Total	464	465	485	Total
Under 18	285	93	11	389	36	13	14	63
18-65	223	153	73	449	200	208	60	468
Over 65	83	82	46	211	58	52	11	121
Total	591	328	130	1,049	294	273	85	652

General points from data

1 Very high school movements, but although they are high in number, fares revenues are small as the distances travelled are very short.

2 Usage overall is poor.

3 Westerham-Crockham Hill section very poorly used.

Progress to date

Kent County Council initiated a revised timetable. The general effect was to reduce evening frequency and virtually withdraw evening journeys in Kent. Certain cuts were made during the day and the result was the saving of one bus on the route, reducing from three to two. The bus used on route 494 now gives assistance to move schoolchildren at peak times.

MB111 passes Brockham Green with a Redhill-bound 425 on 30 August 1979. Buses have tended to serve the A25 route in sections as part of some other routeing, rather than use it in its own right. The problem is that there are too many diversions from which traffic might be gained. *Guy Brigden*

The RNs, high-capacity Plaxton-bodied AEC Reliances with three-plus-two seating acquired from Barton, appeared on local bus routes and the 418 to Kingston was a regular use. RN5 is seen at Great Bookham on 15 April 1978; the narrow gangway resulted from three-plus-two seating, and a single-door layout meant that stop time could be excessive. *Guy Brigden*

Suggested further action

In 1973 school reorganisation in this area will affect the demand for bus services, at which time the situation should be reviewed. The long-term policy could be to consult with Kent CC about discontinuing the service from Surrey into Kent.

London Country Bus Services could then operate one bus between Chart and Holland on an hourly basis, and Kent if needed could perhaps extend a service from Edenbridge to Crockham Hill.

This example shows many of the types of problems which arise and how school movements can completely dominate an operation. At the same time, traditional half fares policies kept the revenue down. This was a group of interworked services which crossed into a neighbouring County, and the wishes of both have to be accommodated in any service revision — provided also that there is a willingness to subvent the operator as necessary. That introduces the need for the division of route-costing between the authorities concerned, and how that should be done. Costs might be apportioned on the basis of mileage within each authority area, but what about revenues? Finally, with the route serviced from Chelsham garage, this accounted for the additional journeys (in service) in that direction, 'making a virtue out of necessity'.

5 County Council responsibilities

'London Country is fortunate in having a realistic attitude to revenue support practised by its Shire County Councils.'

Evidence by NBC and LCBS to the House of Commons Transport Committee, 1981

Over the years, County Councils had had little involvement in the provision of public transport services, other than very remotely in respect of their highways responsibilities. The first major change, and affecting only a limited part of the population, was the passing of the Education Act 1944.

This Act changed the education system for secondary schools in England and Wales. Commonly named after the Conservative politician Rab Butler, it completely reorganised the system of secondary education and made it free for all pupils. Henceforth, there were to be three types of secondary school: grammar, technical and secondary moderns. In practice the number of grammar schools, for the academically inclined, remained unchanged, and few technical schools were ever established. As a result, most pupils went to secondary modern schools, whether they were suitable or not, while most funding went to grammar schools.

The 1944 Act also ended fee-paying for state secondary schools and enforced the division between primary (5-11 year olds) and secondary (11-15 year olds). It also proposed raising the school-leaving age to 16, though this was not followed through until 1972.

The 408 from West Croydon to Guildford was for many years operated by Leyland Atlanteans. AN196 is seen in overall advertising livery for London & Manchester Assurance in suburban Surrey. It is leaving Ewell on a journey back to West Croydon. *John Glover*

An RP in Walthamstow bus station, whose interchange possibilities made it as near an ideal traffic objective for routes from Harlow and that area generally, like the 702, as could be devised. *Barry Le Jeune*

Typically, the new secondary schools were large and drew their pupils from a large catchment area. Walking to the local school was thus often impractical, especially in less-populated areas. From the point of view of transport providers, this had the effect of vastly increasing the demands on their resources for school travel.

But the Education Act had more to say, in support of the commitment that secondary school education should be provided free. The scene was set for the new concept of 'walking distances'. Thus for children who lived more than three miles away from the nearest available school, the Local Education Authority (as part of the County Council) was placed under a duty not only to provide transport, but also to make that provision free of charge to the parent. The statutory distance was reduced to two miles for under eights.

It was up to the authority concerned whether they provided this transport by school contract coaches, or by issuing tickets for travel on ordinary bus (or rail) services; the decision would normally be made on the basis of cost to the authority. It took no account of those whose school was less than the specified distances away; it was up to parents to get these children to school. It was assumed implicitly that they could walk, cycle or use public transport, at their own expense. Being taken to school by car was also of course a possibility, but even by the end of the 1950s there were fewer than five million cars on the road compared with 25million today.

In reality, many would be sent to school by bus, though the fares paid were a constant source of irritation to parents who felt it unfair that some of their child's contemporaries did not have to pay at all. The situation thus created was to cause major problems in the future.

LOCAL GOVERNMENT ACT 1972

Rural bus grants were a means to an end, but, as it turned out, only a temporary expedient. The 1968 and 1969 Acts were responsible for turning over the financing and control of local transport services to the Passenger Transport Authorities in the English Metropolitan areas and the Greater London Council, respectively. What should happen elsewhere, in the shire counties?

The Local Government Act of 1972 provided the Government's answer. The occasion was a major redrawing of the local government map, with new authorities and new duties and powers created.

London Country vehicles (however they might appear!) line up outside Epsom station to take the crowds the mile up the hill to the Derby in 1978. The route is the 406F; suffixes at one time abounded, but the number of variations at one time on the 406 was quite extraordinary. *John Glover*

Local government can only perform functions which it is empowered by Government to undertake, and cannot add to or subtract from them at will. It might perhaps be useful to stress the difference between duties and powers: a 'duty' is something which must be carried out; a 'power' is the legal authority to undertake a function which need only be exercised if the council concerned wishes so to do.

The relevant section of the 1972 Act, Section 203, read as follows:

(1) Within each non-metropolitan county, it shall be the duty —

    (a) of the county council, acting in consultation with persons providing bus services within the county and, so far as appropriate, with the Railways Board, to develop policies which will promote the provision of a co-ordinated and efficient system of public passenger transport to meet the needs of the county and, for that purpose, to take such steps to promote the co-ordination, amalgamation and re-organisation of road passenger undertakings in the county as appears to the county council to be desirable.

    (b) referred to municipal operations, not relevant here.

    (c) of each of the persons providing bus services within the county and of the Railways Board to co-operate with one another in the exercise and performance of their respective functions for the purpose of co-ordinating the passenger transport services within the county and to afford to one another such information as to proposed changes in their services as may be reasonably required for that purpose.

(2) For the purpose of such co-operation as referred to in subsection (1)(c) above, the Railways Board and each of the other persons mentioned in that subsection shall have power to enter into such agreements with one another with respect to the exercise and performance of their respective functions on such terms as may appear to them to be expedient, including arrangements under the Companies Acts of, and the transfer of assets to, one or more companies controlled (severally or jointly) by the parties to the agreements.

The London Transport symbol outline still appears, though that is all. An RF on a Summer Sunday Croydon-Crawley working on the 405 hurries south through Redhill. *John Glover*

(3) The council of a non-metropolitan county… may make grants towards any costs incurred by persons carrying on public passenger transport undertakings wholly or partly in the county…

The County Council's proposals for both revenue and capital expenditure would form part of an annual submission to the Department of Environment under the Transport Policies & Programmes system (TPP). If approved, grants would be paid through the Transport Supplementary Grant (TSG) process which provided approximately 70% of county revenue support. The balance was financed by the counties themselves. Thus only a modest portion of the cost of supporting buses fell on local sources.

The new powers took effect from local government reorganisation in April 1974, though the first year was largely a transitional period during which the new arrangements were put in place and staff appointed.

THE NEW DUTIES

The new duties were extensive, but were considerably limited. There was no transfer of ownership of bus undertakings, unlike the situation in the Passenger Transport Executives (PTEs) at the time, and the operators still obtained Road Service Licences from the Traffic Commissioner in a manner which was completely unchanged.

The Councils, for their part, were to develop policies and co-ordinate the provision, for which they were empowered to make revenue grants to the operators. Capital grants might also be made. One quick response from the County Council officers was to set up the Association of Transport Co-ordinating Officers (ATCO), a professional body through which ideas could be exchanged and the new responsibilities developed.

The Act gave the County Councils the duty of public transport co-ordination, but without any effective method of control over what actually took place, these would have their limitations. There was no hint of any contractual arrangement between the parties. Such agreements were for a later era; at that time it was understood implicitly that the bus companies knew how to run services and would do so in an at least adequate manner.

The County Councils were there to step in to provide additional revenue (hence the term revenue support) for routes they considered should continue to operate for social reasons but the operator was unable to run at a profit. The offer of revenue support was just that; it did not confer any say in whether either Operator's

A smartly turned-out RCL in London Country but non-NBC livery on a 405B at Crawley bus station. *Barry Le Jeune*

licences or Road Service Licences should be amended in any way, or even surrendered. These were still matters for the Traffic Commissioners, a quasi-judicial body, who could determine whether the operator was in breach of its licence conditions.

It followed that the County Councils had no jurisdiction to force an operator to surrender a Road Service Licence should they feel, perhaps, that another operator could provide a similar service more cheaply. They may have been right or wrong, but there was no means of putting it to the test without the full agreement of all concerned.

Thus the situation facing local authorities was that they could make arrangements with operators to pay revenue support, but if the support was withheld or paid at a level less than that demanded, it was in the operator's gift to decide what to do in response. Nationally, there were many instances of local authority payments being very much less than the support demanded, but this did not necessarily lead to service withdrawals.

COSTING OF BUS OPERATIONS

Unsurprisingly, the question arose quickly that if County Councils were empowered to make grants towards the provision of unremunerative bus services, how should the relevant costs and revenues, and hence support required from public funds, be calculated? In those days the costing of bus operations by route was in its infancy, and allocations much below garage level tended to raise as many questions as they answered.

The costs most directly attributable to route level, the variable costs, are relatively simple so to do. These are crew wages and vehicle servicing (based on time), with fuel, tyres and insurance (based on mileage). If the service isn't provided, the costs aren't incurred. Broadly, the variable costs will account for roundly half the total.

Next are the semi-variables of the inspectorate and supervisory staff costs, vehicle maintenance, garage and workshop expenses, all based on time. Other semi-variable costs such as ticket equipment, publicity, vehicle licences, vehicle depreciation and leasing were assigned to the number of peak vehicles employed. This was defined as the maximum number of vehicles required at any one time to meet traffic needs on a route (or group of routes) on local services. These semi-variable costs equate to about a third of the total. By the nature of such costs, they can only be *allocated* to individual routes; to suggest that they will all be saved if a few evening journeys are discontinued is at best wishful thinking.

Finally there are the fixed costs of administrative staff, welfare, rent, buildings maintenance and depreciation, staff vehicles, office expenses and the like, of perhaps a sixth of all expenses. These are all very much in the realm of overheads, and the only way of doing much to these is likely to be relatively drastic in its effects.

So the situation arises that while costs can be allocated down to individual routes, this is far from saying that this is what it costs to run a given route. The actual costs directly attributable will be very much less, but the bus company will still be incurring them — *and they have to be covered somehow*.

Thus, went the argument, local authority support for unremunerative bus services should be based on the total costs of operation allocated down to at least route level. If they are not so covered, they have in effect to be carried by the commercially viable services, which will end up tipping these further towards being loss-making. Another alternative is borrowing, which has its own cost.

The upshot was that the whole subject was thrashed out between the interested parties, and a joint working party was convened under the Chartered Institute of Public Finance and Accountancy (CIPFA). Its recommendations in an undated report around 1973 included the form of a standard financial statement and the elements of a route-costing system. Crucially, though, it recommended the full costing system for general use, while acknowledging that there were situations where a marginal approach should be applied. It was in this way that full route costing became the norm for bus company demands on County Councils.

REVENUES

Revenue allocation has almost as many pitfalls as cost allocation. Where cash single fares are taken on a bus, such revenue is easily credited to that route. The same applies to returns, though modest complications arise if the return part can be used on another service. Likewise, if the driver changes to another route during the shift, the ticket machine readings at the point of change need to be recorded.

Far more problematic are tickets purchased off-bus, or any area-wide tickets which are valid on a number of services and maybe more than one operator. How does one allocate Rover ticket revenue? The revenues from season tickets of any description also have to be allocated, and also that from scholars' term tickets or other local authority sources as compensation for operator participation in concessionary fares schemes.

The theory is straightforward, though its execution can be more difficult. In short, conventions have to be devised on how such tasks should be approached, and then implemented.

The financial situation on any route was calculated as the attributable revenue, net of the attributable costs.

MARGINAL COSTING

Persuasive as the argument for full costing might be, it was by far the end of the story. What happens if a Council pays less than demanded?

That was for the operator to determine. But let us suppose that the amount offered by the Council is sufficient to cover the variable costs of operation and perhaps a chunk of the semi-variables, net of revenue. The less directly associated costs such as garage, workshop, publicity, depreciation and administration expenses will still be outstanding. Such expenditure has to be met, and was indeed included in the CIPFA 'bible' of what were acceptable cost items and how they should be calculated. Even so, in the short term, if as an absolute minimum all the direct operational costs of a route are covered, *the company is still financially better off running that route with less than adequate support, than not running it at all*.

It was however enough to make many Councils wary of paying anything like the amounts demanded, and not without reason. There are occasions where marginal costing is appropriate, as for instance, in vehicles turned out for race meetings to take the crowds to and from the racecourse on a few occasions a year, or additional work undertaken off-peak only using resources which would otherwise be idle, and CIPFA recognised this. But the core business cannot be run on such principles.

Where services are operated commercially without any need for the intervention of outside interests, such cost divisions are of little more than academic interest to outsiders. They take on another slant when the provider needs financial support for their operation. A good reason has to be found if public moneys are to be expended; the discussion earlier of the 464/465/485 service group in the Oxted area demonstrated some early thoughts on such matters.

The Council approach

As the true state of bus company finances gradually unfolded, this inevitably became the focus of early attention. But what did the wider picture look like, and what approach should the County Councils be taking?

That depended on what they were trying to do. Thus Surrey's County Structure Plan, then in the process of being formulated, was at best lukewarm towards bus provision. Policy 44 in the version approved by the Secretary of State in 1980 declared: 'the County Council will seek to retain a bus network for those people dependent on bus services'.

The people referred to were 'those without cars, old age pensioners etc', while 'except where there is an overwhelming social need, patronage must be sufficient to provide a major contribution towards the overall costs of providing services'. It was clear that services catering for journeys to work, school and shopping would be given a higher priority, while the importance of reducing overall operating costs to the minimum possible for the level of service envisaged was also stressed. There was no hint of any chance to affect the modal split of how people travelled, though the Council would introduce highway schemes to reduce delays to buses and improve reliability.

County Council surveys showed generally that people were prepared to walk half a mile to catch a bus.

Surrey of the 1970s was very much a county of motorists. Thus in 1971 only 22% of the adult population had no car. Translated into household terms, 19% of households had two or more cars, 52% had one, and 29% none at all. But were they bus users? There were many matters perceived to be wrong here by the public, as a survey revealed. For one, buses were seen as a declining industry, and services were unreliable. The cost of bus services was perceived as high, whether in terms of the cost of fares for users or support from taxpayers. On the other hand, there was a low level of knowledge of what could reasonably be expected to be provided by public transport, given the various constraints. This was only a few years after the huge uproar created by the railway closures following Dr Beeching's report on railway reshaping of 1963 and its subsequent implementation over the succeeding five years or so.

The general tenor of opinion could not be classified as supportive; if it is more so today, that is a measure of progress made in the intervening years. Nevertheless, such sentiments are of the broad brush type; faced with the loss of large numbers of real bus services for which financial support is needed if they are to be retained, elected Members will tend to be guided on the practical steps that can be taken to retain at least that which is judged worthwhile.

The County Councils were clearly not just going to pay up. At the end of 1974 the relevant Committee in Surrey noted that 'the bus subsidy situation is a matter of urgency. In view of rapidly escalating costs and claims by operators which exceed estimates several-fold, a continuing appraisal of operational effectiveness must be carried out.'

The whole situation had not been helped by the Department of the Environment, whose 1974 projections of the overall sums which would be required for bus revenue support in England and Wales fell from £102million in 1975/76 to £85million in 1976/77 and £50million in 1978/79. If that was going to be the trend in the Transport Supplementary Grant settlements for the County Councils, life was beginning to look even harder.

Quick action?

The financial situation clearly wasn't getting much better, but the lead-time for the introduction of service reductions was a minimum of about six months. Rationalisation of London Country services in Hertfordshire had however reached the point where there was very little remaining slack in the system. Further service cuts

Guildford bus station arrangements are in this 1986 diagram, which shows how the 'saw tooth' arrangement differs from 'straight-through'. *London Country*

Friary Bus Station

Stop Numbers	Services
1	214
2	National Express
3	268. 271
4	274. 292. 294
5	260. 265
6	284. 285. 286. 290
7	G3
8	263. 269. 273. 283. 293. 299
9	G9. G10. G11. G12. G13
10	279. 280. 281
11	G4
12	G5
13	G1 (to Onslow Village)
14	451. 452. 453
15	G2 (to Grange Park)
16	773
17	408 Express
18	G7. G8
19	436. 437. G6
20	710. 713. 715. 740 G1 (to Boxgrove Park) G2 (to Charlotteville)
21	23. 25. 33. 44
22	Bus stand only

FWT 6.1986

would have had to be widespread, would seriously inconvenience the public and would greatly increase the proportion of overheads being carried by the remaining services. The only remaining London Country services which had not been rationalised since 1974 were those in Welwyn Garden City/Hatfield and the Watford area. Studies were urgently put in hand in both. But significant savings were unlikely to be possible without considerable inconvenience to the travelling public.

The introduction of one-man operation had occurred on many routes, and the further scope in Hertfordshire was now very limited. The rate at which it could proceed was in any event related to the availability of suitable vehicles.

THE SUPPORT MECHANISM

The method of providing revenue support had some distinct shortcomings, much of which was to do with timing. County Councils needed estimates from operators to enable them to submit their own bids to the Department of Transport by July 1975. The decisions would be made in December 1975, in respect of the year starting April 1976 and finishing in March 1977. Thus the time from bid to finalisation was approximately 21 months.

Given the volatility of the situation and even allowing some crude corrections for inflation, estimates would vary widely as time progressed. Thus an initial bid by LCBS of £1,097m in Surrey was later recalculated at £786,000, but the final figure was £1,348m. Variations stemmed from too optimistic estimates being made on the effects of massive fare increases, the problems of cost estimation when these were rising at rates of over 20% a year and the value to be put on service economies from whatever date it might possible to implement them. As can be seen, the deficit went down as well as up. Local government finances are no more able to stand such fluctuations as anybody else's, so in the end a compromise had to be reached. What was more, estimates for 1977/78 had to be submitted only three months into the previous financial year, and so it all continued.

It should perhaps be stressed that this is not a criticism of the financial system as such. Rather, it is a recognition that the position in which London Country was placed, with all the other problems surrounding the company, was never going to bring about a straightforward and tidy answer. Other bus operators had similar difficulties.

The overall position of London Country in the years 1976/77 to 1983/84, after the transition year of 1975/76, is shown in the table below:

London Country results in Surrey (only)
1976/77-1983/84

	1976/77	1977/78	1978/79	1979/80	1980/81	1981/82	1982/83	1983/84
Revenue, out-turn £'000	3,716	3,846	4,362	4,774	5,152	5,684	6,140	n/a
Costs, out-turn £'000	5,064	5,640	6,048	6,717	7,382	7,850	8,693	n/a
Deficit, out-turn £'000	1,348	1,794	1,676	1,943	2,230	2,166	2,553	2,628
Revenue support £'000	926	1,015	1,444	1,869	2,195	2,166	2,553	2,605
Revenue support, indexed to RPI, 1976/77=100								
	100	94	125	142	141	124	134	128
Vehicle miles, thousands								
	8,311	7,829	7,981	7,960	7,326	6,534	6,674	6,850
As index, 1976/77=100	100	94	96	96	88	79	77	82
Fares index, 1976/77=100								
	100	121	162	179	226	255	288	310
RPI, 1976/77=100	100	116	125	142	168	188	206	220
Passenger journeys, millions								
	29.0	25.0	24.2	23.2	22.5	19.8	19.3	17.6
As Index, 1976/77=100	100	97	93	90	79	77	75	74

Redhill bus station was a late addition, seen here in December 1987 with South West added to the fleetname of the Leyland National on a 430 to Merstham. *John Glover*

Heavy schools traffic always requires large numbers of vehicles, for which other productive use is often minimal. What is more, schools are only in session for about 192 days a year. Pupils board Leyland Atlantean AN131 on a 468 service to Effingham, while behind others join a hired Bournemouth Corporation vehicle forming a 470 to Dorking. The location is the eastern approach to Leatherhead, where a number of schools are situated. The picture is taken from the footbridge built to allow pupils to cross the road in safety.
John Glover

As can be seen, revenue support in real terms in Surrey climbed considerably until 1979/80, later dropping back as the Council felt the need to make economies. Thus: 'The County Council has sought to give every encouragement to London Country and will continue to do so on the grounds that many of its current problems are not of its making. However, increasing demands for revenue support, coupled with escalating fares and patchy reliability, are causes for concern.' This came from the Transport Policy & Planning submission to the Department for 1979/80.

Vehicle miles stayed up better than might have been expected, but this was due in large part to the extra mileage on acquired routes, offset by economies elsewhere. Passenger journeys disappointed, though, falling back substantially in the inflation round of the early 1980s.

The ebbing of passenger traffic was not something new; London Country provided estimates for Surrey in the last year of London Transport ownership in 1969 of 34.1 million passenger journeys, which had dropped to 32.1 million the following year, the first under NBC.

In the last year of the rural bus grant, Surrey had paid out £66,348 in subsidy.

Hertfordshire used some rather different measures, but the downward provision and usage over time was still very apparent:

London Country in Hertfordshire

	1978/79	1983/84	change %
Vehicle miles per '000 population	17,660	15,773	-10.7%
Passenger journeys per '000 population	56,911	48,240	-15.2%

LONDON COUNTRY'S VIEW

What was the company's view? The following came from Derek Fytche, Managing Director of LCBS, in 1980.

'We start from the point, in our discussions with the county, of having assessed the market which the public would need for the purposes of their own mobility. From that, we then produce plans which would provide services which in our view, and the public's view generally, are precisely what they want.

The extension of the 412 from Dorking through to Cranleigh was justified on the basis of the schools traffic it could take off contract vehicles, but other traffic did not materialise in the quantities which had been hoped. This was 1980, when a better service was provided than for many years previously. *John Glover*

'The county will then take a view on the amount of money that is needed in order to finance that particular network of services, and the amount of money that can be put in from public funding and the amount that can be raised from fares.

'It is at that point that one has to take into account the county views in regard to the provision of public transport. It is the eternal triangle — on one side you have the cost of operating the network, on the other you have income and fares, joined together by that strand at the bottom, which is public funding. There is a considerable difference in philosophy and policy within all nine county councils, and what we do then is to find the best arrangement of services, given those county plans or county attitudes.

'There are examples in every instance of cross boundary services disputed between counties. Thus LCBS has services going from Hertfordshire into Buckinghamshire, travelling through relatively semi-urban areas, where there is discord as to whether it is needed in precisely that form. It is not whether the public need it; it is whether there is enough money available in the budget to meet that difference between fares income and the actual cost of operation.'

Performance

What did the County Councils do about London Country's poor operational performance in those early years? Put more bluntly, what could they do? The answer in both cases was very little, though the effects on the quality of service provision and hence on the passengers was often nothing short of disastrous.

Physically, there was no practical help they could offer, but it was recognised that the problems were not of the company's making. Probably the worst possible response would have been to cut back severely on revenue support payments, which would have added yet further financial woes to what was already a very difficult situation.

It would seem that the company managed to retain the support of most, if not all, the Councils during this period. Should the County Councils have helped to finance the Crawley Works? The suggestion met with a stiff response from Hertfordshire's County Secretary in a letter to Essex County Council on 2 December 1975:

'The provision, operation, servicing arrangements and garaging of the buses is the prerogative of the operator and where this involves revenue or capital expenditure, it is up to him to finance it and, presumably, when operating on a full cost basis, to take it into account when lodging claims for unremunerative working against the County Councils.'

It was still early days in the new relationship, and the response might have been more amenable later. Kent County Council, for instance, made a contribution towards the costs of modernising Dartford Garage. Even so, asking County Councils, including some north of the Thames, to contribute to the building of an engineering base in the Gatwick area over which they would have no control at all, did strain the credibility a little.

LONDON COUNTRY AND LONDON

In 1980, 10 years after becoming part of the NBC, London Country was still providing approximately 5% of the capital's bus mileage. Broadly, the role of London Country and Green Line as they affected Londoners were:

- Provision of local transport for shopping and social needs in GLC fringe areas, such as Bexleyheath, Orpington, Croydon, Kingston, Uxbridge, Enfield and Romford. Further afield, it was also the principal operator in the New Towns largely populated by resettled Londoners
- Commuter transport for those living outside the GLC area but working in central London or developed commercial centres such as Croydon. A proportion of commuters were taken directly to central London by Green Line coach, but the majority were carried on feeder services to principal stations, whether British Rail or Underground. These included Orpington, Epsom, Redhill, Woking, Slough, Watford, St Albans, Hatfield, Harlow and Walthamstow
- Orbital connections between one part of the GLC outer area and another, not provided by the Underground or the shorter-distance red buses. The prime example was the Green Line 725 which was established as early as 1953 and the later 726 across the spine between Gravesend and Windsor. Although their termini were in the Home Counties, most of the routes were in Greater London
- Airport links provided by Green Line for businessmen, holidaymakers and incoming tourists. As well as connecting central London with Heathrow, Green Line provided fast inter-airport connections by orbital routes, avoiding the need to travel via central London
- Tourist services, enabling seasonal visitors to London to reach attractions such as Windsor, Hampton Court, Thorpe Park, Chartwell, St Albans, Woburn Abbey and Whipsnade Zoo cheaply, quickly and comfortably. The Green Line name was well known and marketed throughout Europe and in North America.

Relationships with London Transport were particularly important as about 20% of total LCBS vehicle mileage was operated within Greater London. A fares and services agreement dating from 1976 between LTE and LCBS provided for green buses and Green Line coaches to operate on routes within the GLC on routes with frequency and fares agreed by negotiation with LT. The aim of the agreement was to provide best value for money services.

The 1980 plans of LT to introduce a flat-fare system for outer London provided an example. On shared or parallel sections of route within this area, London Country agreed to adjust fares accordingly. This did however create a threat to some Green Line routes, where some long-distance journeys were possible within the flat-fare zone, but an element of market pricing was introduced under the 1976 agreement to preserve profitability. Thus the company effectively acted as a contractor to London Transport, providing services at agreed levels, frequency, quality and fares.

BUS STATIONS

A facility to help bus passengers, for bus operators, a civic benefit to enhance the standing of the town as a whole, or merely a means of getting stationary buses off the streets, where they are deemed a nuisance? In reality, a well-situated and well-designed bus station has benefits in all these areas, but that does raise the question of who should pay for the land, the construction and then the upkeep of the facility.

Thus Surrey County Council paid much of the fitting-out costs for the new Staines and Guildford bus stations, both of which were on development sites, in the case of Guildford on the Friary Brewery site.

Guildford was one of those towns where bus terminating facilities were less than adequate. Alder Valley used two by now shabby bus stations, at Farnham Road and Onslow Street, while most London Country routes

London Country buses of a multitude of descriptions await the end of the Derby on the edge of Epsom Downs, as they prepare to take the passengers back down to Epsom town on the 406F racedays-only service.
Author's collection

were confined to a very basic facility in Commercial Road. The redevelopment of the well-placed site was an opportunity, and it was possible to accommodate all the 57 routes then terminating in Guildford there, including those of the independent operators.

But these things are never as straightforward as they seem. The bus stands were arranged in a 'saw tooth' arrangement so that buses faced the undercover pedestrian waiting and circulating area at a slight angle and a boarding area was created at each stand for passengers, giving easy access. Passengers do not need to spill onto the roadway, as with a series of 'straight-through' stands. It does mean however that buses need to back out, an acceptable arrangement in an area used by buses only and from which pedestrians are excluded.

But it was not acceptable to London Country. That company's buses thus continued to use longitudinal stands, which had to be created away from the main terminal. 'We've always done it that way' was perhaps true, but was it good enough in an industry where traditional methods and ideas were often uppermost in people's minds? This was in 1980, but all-embracing change in the sense of bus deregulation was then still a few years away.

In a more generous layout used at the new Staines bus station (1979), there was no difficulty in providing an ordinary side loading arrangement and it was also found possible to make a more suitable bus terminating arrangement in the railway station forecourt, a short distance east of the town centre.

MOVING FORWARD

There were clearly still problems in the legislative background, which later gave rise to the Transport Act 1978. This strengthened the position of the County Councils, in that they were now required to produce an annual Public Transport Plan (from 1979/80) setting out a review of the county's public transport needs and the criteria used in determining them. This would formally set out the county's policies and objectives, how they intended to secure them, and an estimate of the financial resources needed. They were also to enter into agreements with operators on the securing of unremunerative services.

There was a revision of the criteria used for the issue of Road Service Licences by the Traffic Commissioners, in that they were obliged to take heed of any aspects of the new Public Transport Plans which were drawn to their attention by the authority concerned. County Councils could also give evidence on their views of the adequacy (or otherwise) of existing services in the area.

Further relaxation in the Road Service Licence conditions took place under the Transport Act 1980, which also saw the coaching market freed from all such constraints and the effective abolition of fares control.

6 Strategy and execution

'Reconnaissance is never wasted.'

Donald Allison, Public Transport Co-ordinator, Surrey County Council

CONTAINING THE SITUATION

The developing situation produced a thoughtful paper from Hertfordshire. Written in mid-1975 or thereabouts, it encapsulated the situation in the counties neatly:

'The unpalatable conclusion is that if bus services are to be maintained at anything near their present level the majority of services will always make a loss, and that their maintenance can only be achieved by financial support from Central and Local Government resources, probably on a scale considerably higher than at present.

London Transport Bristol LH BL80 on the 237 from Hounslow to Chertsey station has just crossed Chertsey Bridge. Chertsey would soon be a terminus no more for the red buses, which were about to begin a phased partial withdrawal from Surrey. *John Glover*

It is June 1973 and the 711 Green Line service to High Wycombe, operated by a Leyland National coach (SNC) outside Reigate Garage would later be withdrawn. In replacement, a new local service of 420 and 422 would operate south from Sutton, allowing various London Transport routes to be curtailed. *Barry Le Jeune*

It is fundamental that efforts must be made to establish relative priorities and to facilitate rational and informed decisions to be taken.' A possible scenario followed:

- Withdrawal of Green Line routes throughout Hertfordshire
- Withdrawal of a small number of other little used routes
- Reduction of services where some form of reasonable alternative exists
- Pruning of rural services to a level which will maintain a basic minimum network sufficient to provide reasonable services for journeys to work and a non-peak service of at least one return bus a day

and

- Retention of routes with a potential for revenue increase in relation to the size of their catchment areas. These would be likely to be mainly in towns and would include the small number of routes which are at the moment profit making
- Retention of routes serving centres of employment and shopping which are likely to expand
- Retention of inter-related town networks which will provide a basis on which to build improved services
- Retention of routes serving concentrations of the old, the young and the poor, if these can be identified

Stress was put on the need for further on-bus surveys, to enable knowledge to be built up of what was happening out on the road, whilst the potential for differential fares policies was canvassed.

Surrey also showed a deal of pragmatism. The objectives in 1976 were seen as:

1 Provision of a county transportation system that meets the needs (and wherever possible the wishes) of the people, taking account of:
   a) attitudes of people and operators towards public transport
   b) levels of service required for particular areas of the county
   c) fares to be charged, methods of collection
   d) availability of resources
   e) need for industry to offer worthwhile and stable employment to staff

2 To help put right the financial plight of operators

3 Provision of reliable services with proper co-ordination between various modes

4 Promotion of policies that would enable highway and traffic management schemes to take account of the needs of public transport as well as lorry and private car.

ACTION ON ALL FRONTS

The type of situation which arose was demonstrated in a letter from the LCBS Operating Manager to Hertfordshire County Council on 1 December 1975. It set out the state of play reached on no fewer than 48 different routes (or groups of routes) in the County. This would involve the withdrawal of a total of 10 peak vehicles from Garston, Hemel Hempstead and Hertford garages, which was proposed for the following spring.

This is a long list, but it is perhaps worth quoting a selection of items:

301/302	The present timetable will be adjusted to re-route 301 via Hemel Hempstead town centre and to withdraw 302 between Bennetts Gate and Marlowes
308	Saturday service will be reduced to four journeys
315	Awaiting recommendations from County
322/A	Journey reduction will be implemented in accordance with the increased vehicle capacity proposed; off peak headways will become 30 minute, increasing to 20 minute. The Sunday service on Route 322A will be withdrawn
350/351	The service will be withdrawn between Hertford and Potters Bar/New Barnet, except for three off-peak journeys between Hertford and Essendon
381/384	County to liaise with Lister Hospital about the withdrawal of evening and Sunday services. No alteration to present Stevenage-Letchworth service until County have produced firm recommendation about the future of Route 383. Journeys to Great Munden will be curtailed at Dane End
382	LCBS will obtain current loadings to support complete withdrawal of service
387	LCBS will obtain loadings, but it is doubtful whether any material saving would be achieved except by complete withdrawal. County should therefore examine cost benefit implications of withdrawal of the public transport link between Tring town and station, and possible alternative means of providing a service
716/A	Some urgent action is required in view of the heavy losses being sustained on this service, and I propose to implement a revised hourly service from Hitchin via 716 to Welwyn Garden City, then via 716A to Woking, which combines the more remunerative sections of each route
803	I cannot support the recommendation to terminate the service in central Watford, as carryover traffic (those passengers whose journeys cross the town centre) at this point forms a significant part of the total patronage. Furthermore, I am in some difficulty recommending a morning peak reduction, as each vehicle performs a well used journey either towards Hatfield or across St Albans to Watford, and no vehicle saving can be achieved by terminating at Watford in the morning. It is possible that an economy can be secured from reductions to other services in the Watford area which will assist in a vehicle saving were the evening peak 803 service to be reduced, and I will advise you further.

The situation was similar all over the London Country area and in many ways it was a continuous feature of life in the mid-1970s and beyond. The picture emerges of extensive co-operation between the company and the County Councils, each with their own objectives and resources, but with an overriding need to stem any waste resulting from operations where patronage was poor. But the approach was also tinged with reality, as for instance in the discussion on the 803. Reducing service provision to save expenditure is understandable, but not if the traffic which provides the income ebbs away even faster.

In the Banstead area reorganisation, London Transport's 80 would soon be terminating in the Greater London areas, in this case at Belmont station. Bristol LH BL84 provides the service. *John Glover*

EXTENT OF THE PROBLEM

The problems facing both London Country and Surrey County Council in 1976/77 were daunting, with few easy options open to either party. Financially, only the following routes were returning what might be considered a reasonable cost recovery ratio of 75%, or more:

403	Warlingham Park Hospital-Croydon-Wallington
405	West Croydon-Redhill-Crawley
406	Kingston-Epsom-Redhill
408	West Croydon-Epsom-Guildford
408A	Guildford-Merrow, Bushey Hill Estate
409	West Croydon-Godstone-East Grinstead-Forest Row
410	Reigate-Bromley
411	West Croydon-Godstone-Reigate
414	West Croydon-Reigate-Horsham
420	Woking-West Byfleet
430	Redhill-Earlswood-Reigate
436	Staines-Addlestone-Woking-Guildford
441/C/D	Staines-Windsor-High Wycombe
461	Staines-Addlestone-Walton-on-Thames
463	Walton-on-Thames-Woking-Guildford
470	West Croydon-Epsom-Dorking
483	West Croydon-Westerham-Tonbridge
705	Sevenoaks-Victoria-Windsor
715	Guildford-Oxford Circus- Hertford
724	Romford-Heathrow Airport-Staines Express
725	Gravesend-Kingston-Windsor
727	Luton Airport-Heathrow Airport-Gatwick Airport-Crawley Express

These were in essence the main trunk routes, with only three which might be counted as urban services (408A, 420, 430), and none at all for anything even vaguely rural. Thus only 22 out of around 70 routes operated by London Country wholly or partly in Surrey were in anything like good financial shape.

Besides revisions to rural services, there had already been painstaking attempts to remove surplus peak-hour capacity, and hence vehicles, wherever possible, and other 'good housekeeping'-type curtailments at the ends of the working day or at weekends. It might stretch to all-day frequency reductions. A list similar to the Hertfordshire changes could have been repeated in Surrey, and no doubt in the other counties too.

There was clearly a long and hard road ahead. Throughout, individually modest but overall substantial cuts would continue.

SURREY STRATEGY

The Surrey strategy which developed had essentially two elements. The first was to replan the existing services to provide a more economical service in line with passenger requirements. The second, perhaps more controversially, was to replace higher-cost operators with lower-cost ones.

There were good reasons for thinking that economies might be possible, and the table below gives details:

**Table: The three major Surrey operators compared
1976/77 prices**

	London Transport	London Country	Alder Valley*
Average costs per bus mile	83.9p	59.6p	48.7p
Average revenue per bus mile	39.2p	46.8p	38.5p
Average deficit per bus mile	44.7p	12.8p	14.2p

* The second Surrey NBC subsidiary based in Aldershot, but not operating generally east of Guildford/Woking.

Such statistics should not be taken as telling the whole tale; for one thing, London Transport's revenue was lower as they pursued a fares policy more generous to the passengers, though this was changing. Similarly, Alder Valley's staff costs were lower, reflecting rates of pay. What was unmistakable in all the analysis carried out was that London Transport was by far the most expensive operator and, as far as could be judged, likely to remain so.

This therefore gave rise to an exercise to see whether Surrey's dependence on LT could be lessened. At this time, London Transport operated a quarter of the bus mileage in Surrey, but at a deficit equal to that of London Country and Alder Valley combined for the remaining three quarters. London Country passenger journeys in Surrey were then roundly 28.7million a year, producing a revenue of £4.0m. This resulted in a deficit of 3.8p per passenger journey, or 12.8p per bus mile operated as shown above.

Assuming the idea was practicable, could it be achieved? What benefits did Surrey stand to gain? It was already clear that London Country was the only organisation capable of taking on such work in the volumes which were likely to be required.

The main benefit to Surrey was the potentially lesser cost of operation, but the effects were rather more complex. It was already clear that the garages operated in Surrey by London Country (then eight) were becoming an increasing drain on company resources because of falling workloads over the years. By moving more work into them, the garage overheads would become more manageable in terms of the cost per vehicle. While it was true that an equal and opposite effect would take place with London Transport, this was not a County Council concern. Even for those who deplore such calculations, the financial imperatives were such that benefits of this nature could not be ignored.

There was no reason, at least in principle, why London Country should not provide at least as satisfactory a service for the passenger as London Transport. Both had suffered from the supply industry problems of late.

Could it be achieved? This was a more difficult question to answer, since it was operators who held Road Service Licences and not the County Council. While it would be possible to approach London Transport on a 'we shan't pay you, so go away' basis, the results from such an action could never be very satisfactory. Services could be withdrawn in such a way that made it very difficult for them to be replaced on anything like a

Edgware Borehamwood
Arkley Barnet
Oakwood Enfield
Southbury Station

EDGWARE STN

107

SHOP EARLY BY DAY

NLP 519

London Transport's services went into many of the shire counties, in the case of the 107, into Hertfordshire and out again later. Boundaries were not designed around public transport; the RT4354, with roof box, is heading for Edgware. *John Glover*

satisfactory basis, but in any event London Transport held a trump card. This was the section of the 1969 Act which required any company which wished to operate in Greater London to first come to an agreement with London Transport. Who would pay for any operating deficits incurred within Greater London? Would standard London Transport fares and conditions of travel apply? Could a suitable terminating point be found?

No agreement? No operation.

It was clear that any such agreements would only be made by careful preparation of the ground but also the presenting of schemes which were both well thought-out and met the apparent needs of Greater London passengers as well. This could only be achieved over a number of years.

A number of the service revisions which took place in respect of both parts of Surrey's strategy are discussed below. To support them, detailed on-bus surveys were continued with the help of what was by now the ageing Surrey caravan.

237 Hounslow-Feltham-Sunbury-Shepperton-Chertsey

This was the first move in Surrey to cut back the operation of London Transport services, in this case from Chertsey to Sunbury Village. The 237 wound its way from Hounslow through Greater London until it entered Surrey a little short of Sunbury Cross. It then proceeded to the Thames at Lower Sunbury, then west to Shepperton and Chertsey Bridge.

The replacement devised, LCBS 459, was to run from Addlestone garage, north to Chertsey and thence by the same route, terminating at Feltham Station. Meanwhile, the 237 would be truncated at Lower Sunbury and was extended back to Shepherds Bush.

This revision took effect in January 1978. Another early change was the pulling back of LT services to Egham and terminating them in Staines.

417 Ramblers' Bus

Amid the gloom of service economies which became a permanent feature of life in this era, some positive developments were achieved. It had long been the situation that the area of the greensand hills to the south-west of Dorking and south of the A25 were choked with visitors on fine summer days. However, access by public transport was non-existent.

The concept developed in terms of what could be achieved with one bus and one driver on a summer Sunday. What became the 417 was to be aimed at non-car owners, and would provide access to areas such as the bottom of Leith Hill, Holmbury Hill and the Tillingbourne Valley. This evolved into a round trip from Dorking in one direction only at a flat fare. North of Dorking, the road to Ranmore on the North Downs would also be served.

Who would operate it? There were no independents in the area, and London Country had a garage in Dorking. Most of the roads used (61%) were covered during the week by its own 412 service. London Country's operation thus became a *de facto* conclusion. Back-up facilities were also available, if required. Train connections would be made at Dorking North station, and also with 714 Green Line; Golden Rover bus/coach tickets would be accepted.

What though of the finances? This was a case where marginal costing could reasonably be applied, and London Country agreed so to do. Bus operation would cost £20 per day for the 1977 summer season. A substantial publicity effort was made, and both the Youth Hostels Association and the Ramblers Association newsletters carried details. The County Council set a maximum of £500 that they were prepared to underwrite for the 16 days of operation from the start on 5 June 1977, including the August Bank Holiday.

The results were deemed very satisfactory. This was a new service in an atmosphere of financial problems and general decline. Up to 44 passengers were being carried at a time on the Bank Holiday. On-bus revenue was worth £168.63, and another £100.80 was allocated from off-bus revenue (Rovers bought on other services). At a total cost of £320, the loss came to £50.57, or £3.16 per day of operation.

It was agreed that the Ranmore leg, which few patronised, would not be included in the 1978 programme.

Above: The substitution of the 215 with Green Line 715 meant the latter diverting into Cobham High Street. It is seen here with an RP on a Kingston-only journey. *John Glover*

Right: The 417 Ramblers' Bus was a leisure facility introduced to give access into recreation areas, in this case behind Dorking. It is seen here with a well-filled RF at Dorking North. *Barry Le Jeune*

With this amendment to the timetable, Ramblers' Bus ran again in 1978 but for 25 days, when passenger traffic nearly trebled and it made a profit of £153.

It was repeated in a number of subsequent years. The financial figures have been included as they illustrate the very different price levels of 30 years ago. They also put into context the extent of the huge deficit with which all County Councils were burdened in these years, discussed elsewhere.

224 Uxbridge-West Drayton-Poyle-Staines-Laleham

This unlikely route replaced the two railway branch lines from West Drayton & Yiewsley to Uxbridge Vine Street and to Staines West. They closed in 1962 and 1965 respectively.

The route to Laleham was an early casualty of County Council economies, and the 224 was cut back to run from the north to the Poyle Industrial Trading Estate only in 1976, and with a very limited service at that. It was withdrawn totally in Surrey in 1978. A new 451 service operated by London Country's Staines garage replaced the 224 between Staines and Laleham and provided access to the Health Centre.

Further north there was, however, a problem, as a little less than a mile of the old Bath Road (once the A4), including Poyle, was in Surrey. There was now no way of getting by public transport to the nearest Surrey centre of Staines by public transport on anything like a direct route. It might be added that housing is negligible in the intervening area, which consists mostly of reservoirs and, nowadays, the M25. Poyle did however benefit from a regular east-west 81 Hounslow-Slough service provided by LT.

The officers were asked to investigate the provision of a new service linking Poyle with Staines, and hence a shopping service, also operating from London Country's Staines garage as route 467, was suggested as a short-term experiment. It would run at a 90min headway, off-peak only, and the costs which would have to be met were £7,250 per year or £140 per week. A door-to-door leaflet drop was arranged. The service began in November 1976.

The reality was that the average weekly fares income was £25. It was used by five passengers on a sample Monday, three on Tuesday, six on Wednesday, and 11 on each of Thursday and Friday. Saturday really brought them out, and 27 were recorded. That gained a reprieve of the Saturday service for a further year, but that was it. The 467 was not heard of again.

One could say that at least we tried, though in reality there was little to bring people to Staines from a distance, given the other alternatives available. Perhaps the real curiosity was the inclusion of Poyle in Surrey in the first place, but it would take a formal boundary change to make any difference. Many years later, that is exactly what happened.

206 Claygate-Esher-Hampton Court
215 Kingston-Cobham-Downside
415 Guildford-Ripley
715 Guildford-Kingston bypass-Oxford Circus-Hertford

There was a time when the services on the route between Kingston and Guildford (the old A3) were provided by bus 215 and Green Line 715. However, the paucity of traffic in the centre section resulted in the 215 being cut back to Ripley and then to Cobham with, for a time, a route diversion to terminate at Downside, a small village a mile south of Cobham. A 415 route was introduced from the Guildford end to serve the section to Ripley.

However, the route was still over-provided; what could be done to offer a service at lower cost? In many ways, making use of the 715 Green Line seemed most appropriate, since the limited-stop nature was of little

The Rambler Bus 417 promotional poster produced by London Country, featuring a Bristol LH rather than an RF. *John Glover*

consequence given the long stretches with no effective traffic, and it was already in existence. However, it was necessary to divert coaches into the town centre proper.

Against Green Line was the reliability problem on routes of that length which included central London, and that its then routeing was via the Kingston bypass rather than Kingston itself.

The ultimate decision was:

206 Withdrawn; the only London Transport route to run entirely in Surrey

215 Shortened to run between Kingston and Esher only, but diverted to serve Claygate *en route* to Esher, covering the southern part of the 206. Certain journeys extended from Esher to Lower Green on old 206 route for school purposes only

415 Withdrawn between Send and Ripley

710 New peak-hour-only limited-stop route to run from Guildford via Kingston bypass to Oxford Circus

715 Route retained but diverted to run via Kingston centre

MV2 Independent operator Mole Valley Transport Services to run a minibus service between Downside and Cobham (and thence to Leatherhead).

This series of service revisions, which took place over a period, demonstrates how often they are of a cumulative nature and may also be affected by external circumstances. In this case, there were three pairs of bus stops for the 715 on the A3 west of Cobham, which was being rebuilt into the new A3. The highway engineers wanted to remove all of them in the course of road widening, and in two cases loading surveys did not support their retention. However, the third was that for the Royal Horticultural Society's Wisley Gardens. This was well used and a footbridge was built across what was now a six-lane road, with bus lay-bys, to serve it.

The major part of these changes took place on 2 April 1977.

406 Kingston-Tolworth-Ewell-Epsom-Tadworth-Reigate-Redhill
418 Kingston-Surbiton-Berrylands-Tolworth-West Ewell-Epsom-Leatherhead-Bookham

These two long-standing and important London Country routes both provided services between Kingston and Epsom, whereupon they split. However, an early problem identified was the length of time the 418 took to reach Tolworth from Kingston, at 25min compared with 15min on the 406. Although both points are outside Surrey, this meant that journeys between (say) West Ewell and Kingston were inordinately slow. The first move by Surrey County Council was therefore to persuade London Country (and London Transport) to serve the Berrylands Estate in some other way and run the 418 via the main road. The Surbiton station diversion remained, but that was both useful and had only minor effects on timings.

The service was being run at four buses per hour on the 406 with alternate journeys proceeding beyond Tadworth. It was felt that a number of service improvements could be made which could be combined with economies in provision. The opportunity came with the proposed conversion of the 406 from Routemaster RMC to omo in 1978.

This was a limited reshuffle of the 418, which was to be replaced by three new services, 476, 478 and 479. The four routes would combine to offer a 10min service from Kingston to Epsom via the various routes, to be described. The new services started on 28 October 1978.

Apart from omo conversion, the principal revision to the 406 was the reduction of one bus per hour from four to three, with the loss of one of the Redhill journeys beyond Tadworth. However, Epsom retained its six buses per hour, with the three 418 replacement routes each offering an hourly departure instead of the two buses per hour by the 418:

- Kingston-Tolworth-West Ewell-Longmead Road-Epsom-Langley Vale
- Kingston-Tolworth-West Ewell-Hook Road-Epsom-Leatherhead-Bookham Station
- Kingston-Tolworth-West Ewell-Hook Road-Epsom-The Wells Estate-Leatherhead-Preston Cross-Bookham Station

The 476 allowed new housing on the Longmead Estate to be served and the service was extended to Langley Vale; the 419 was withdrawn. Langley Vale thus gained a through route to Kingston. The continued routeing of the 478 and 479 via Hook Road ensured that St Ebba's Hospital on the route retained a service, as well as the housing nearer Epsom.

On the far side of Epsom, the Wells Estate, like Langley Vale, gained a through service from the 479 to both Kingston and Leatherhead and the 481 local town service was withdrawn. As there is only one entry/exit to the Wells Estate, this diversion, plus the later routing via Preston Cross, translated a 20/40min frequency of the 478/479 leaving Epsom to a 29/31min frequency by the time of arrival at Bookham. The effect on London Buses-operated services was additional work only, to serve Berrylands.

At deregulation these services remained initially in a similar form, though some further economies were made. The 476 to Langley Vale was cut back to Epsom but the 478 became the only service to be projected beyond Leatherhead garage to run to Bookham via both Fetcham and Preston Cross. The 479 was rerouted via Longmead Road and ran to Leatherhead garage only. All 406 journeys terminated at Tadworth.

The pattern of six London Country (South West) buses an hour leaving Kingston was thus retained, although there was another change. London Buses decided to register a 306 route, running every half hour but with no evening or Sunday service, on the same route as the 406 and between Kingston and Epsom only. This proved to be relatively short-lived.

464 Holland-Chart
465 Village Bus

London Country's 464, which it was hoped to reduce to a one-bus operation (see Chapter 4), had in the end to be kept at two buses during the peak, mainly for the substantial numbers of schoolchildren. The route however was severely truncated to run only as shown above but with an hourly service and approaching half-hourly at peaks, albeit with various school journeys added on.

The total journey length of the revised 464 was about six miles, with the town centre situated roughly mid-way. Between the settlements the area is entirely rural; as a result, nearly all journeys were about three miles in length. Oxted has a population of around 5,000 and there were two trunk public transport routes — the rail service operating north/south and the 410 bus operating east-west between Reigate and Bromley.

The need to maintain two peak vehicles on the 464 meant that one of the two vehicles was left spare during the day. It was decided to experiment by running this as a shopping service to serve different communities on Tuesdays, Thursdays and Fridays. There would be separate services for Chalkpit Wood, for Tatsfield and Biggin Hill, for Crockham Hill and for Tandridge. This became service 465.

The timetable was constructed as follows:

465 Oxted Village Bus timetable, 1976

	Tuesday, Friday	Thursday
Oxted dep	09.52	09.52
Chalkpit Wood arr	09.57	09.57
Chalkpit Wood dep	09.57	09.57
Oxted arr	10.02	10.02
Oxted dep	10.02	10.02
Tatsfield Ship	10.16	10.16
Biggin Hill PO arr	10.29	10.29
Biggin Hill PO dep	10.31	10.31
Tatsfield Ship	10.41	10.41
Oxted arr	10.55	10.55
Oxted dep	10.55	11.09
Tandridge School arr	11.09	
Tandridge School dep	11.11	
Crockham Hill arr		11.24
Crockham Hill dep		11.26
Oxted arr	11.23	11.41
Oxted dep	11.41	11.41
Chalkpit Wood arr	11.46	11.46
Chalkpit Wood dep	11.46	11.46
Oxted arr	11.51	11.51
Oxted dep	12.14	12.14
Tatsfield Ship	12.29	12.29
Biggin Hill PO arr	12.41	12.41
Biggin Hill PO dep	12.43	12.43
Tatsfield Ship	12.53	12.53
Oxted arr	13.07	13.07
Oxted dep	13.07	13.19
Tandridge School arr	13.19	
Tandridge School dep	13.21	
Crockham Hill arr		13.34
Crockham Hill dep		*13.34*
Oxted arr	13.25	*13.46*

The timetable gave the shopper 1hr 40min in Oxted, give or take a minute or two, which seems about right for a town of Oxted's size. It also shows how the timings are balanced to ensure that the times of the main services do not vary according to day of the week.

Both the 464 and the 465 were made the subject of fares experiments. That for the 464 was a maximum off-peak fare, equal to that for a one-mile journey (11p at the beginning). The intention was to establish whether a reduced fare would generate an increase in the number of journeys made and, if so, whether the fares receipts would be enough to increase total revenue.

The experiment started on 4 September 1976. Over the next two years to 1978, the fare reduction generated 34,000 passenger journeys, a 35% increase. However, it was judged to have reduced revenue by around £1,500 per annum.

Above: The roads at Coldharbour can be exceptionally busy on summer Sundays; this is the scene outside The Plough as the Ramblers' Bus arrives. *Brian Garrard*

Below: The same scene during the week is positively tranquil as the Royal Mail Post Bus passes on one of its three return journeys a day, but during the week only. The 433 service on this road was withdrawn in London Transport days. *John Glover*

Ex-Barton AEC Reliance RN1 works the 422, the 711 replacement service, in Banstead on 15 July 1978. *Guy Brigden*

The 465 single fare was set at 15p for a journey which might be as long as six miles, though that for Chalkpit Wood, which was very much nearer, was set at 7p. Fares were later increased in similar proportions to rises in other fares, but remained considerably less expensive on a distance basis.

An average of 63 passenger journeys a day were made on the 465 during 1977; this fell to 54 during 1978 when higher fares were charged. In view of the level of service offered, this represented a not unsatisfactory level of usage at about 8,000 journeys per annum.

The overall results were:

1978/79	464	465	total
	£	£	£
Annual costs	70,700	6,000	76,700
Annual revenue	29,300	1,900	31,200
Deficit	41,400	4,100	45,500

By 1980, the whole had been reduced to a one-bus operation.

408 West Croydon-Wallington-Sutton-Ewell-Epsom-Leatherhead-Effingham-Guildford
470 West Croydon-Wallington-Sutton-Ewell-Epsom-Leatherhead-Mickleham-Dorking

These were again long-distance routes of long standing, though it was felt that they were not attaining their full potential. The revision of services in this area — a scheme of much wider implications — centred around a complete revamp of the core 408/470 routes from West Croydon to Effingham and Guildford (408) and Dorking (470).

On 17 June 1972, the 408/470 were converted from crew to Atlantean omo and the section to Warlingham Park Hospital (east of Croydon) was withdrawn. In a typical cost-cutting exercise by the company, services were also reduced to four buses per hour Monday-Friday peak Leatherhead-Croydon, and Saturdays to three buses per hour Epsom-Croydon.

The 408/470 were run as an integrated service with three buses an hour at 20min headway as far as

Leatherhead, then an hourly 408 to Guildford, followed by an hourly short working of the 408 to Effingham (giving a 20/40 min frequency to that point), then the hourly service on the 470 to Dorking. The whole was operated from London Country's Leatherhead garage.

The proposal was to make these services limited-stop in the sense of achieving as fast an end-to-end timing as possible. These are long routes with substantial vehicle requirements; Croydon to Epsom is eight miles, Epsom to Leatherhead four miles, Leatherhead to Guildford 12 miles and Leatherhead to Dorking four miles. Journey times were correspondingly long at 116min from West Croydon to Guildford and 90min to Dorking.

The original aspirations for an express service at a half-hourly headway on each route had to be watered down in the light of a detailed examination of passenger loadings, but the plan emerged as a reduction to two buses an hour from Croydon serving, alternately, Effingham only and Guildford. The end-to-end journey time came down to 100min, with buses calling only at those stops carrying a 408 Express designation. The 470 Dorking service was abandoned, apart from a couple of school journeys.

This presaged a substantial revamp of other services in the area. These concerned:

- 265 which ran along the main road from Kingston via Chessington Zoo to Leatherhead, terminating there
- 403 Warlingham Park Hospital-Wallington
- 416 which ran from the community at the top of Boxhill to Leatherhead and thence via Oxshott to Esher
- 419 Epsom town route to Brettgrave
- 432 from Guildford, which negotiated a somewhat tortuous route to serve places off the main road such as Horsley and terminated at Great Bookham
- 468 Epsom-Chessington Zoo via Ewell
- 714 Green Line from Dorking via Leatherhead and Chessington Zoo to London Victoria.

As finally implemented, the revision of services was extensive.

To maintain adequate capacity on the 408/470 section within Greater London, the 403 service was enhanced to four buses per hour east of West Croydon, with two buses per hour running to Wallington station and two buses per hour through to Cheam.

At the western end of the 408, the terminating of the hourly 432 route from Guildford at Great Bookham had always seemed curious, but what alternatives were there? Earlier survey results provided the answer; the 416 from Boxhill was reasonably well used as far as the northern end of the built-up area of Leatherhead, but the section thence to Oxshott and Esher had very sparse patronage. The result was the creation of a new hourly 416 between Boxhill and Guildford, diverted in central Leatherhead via Fetcham to Bookham. The Fetcham routeing enabled the new 416 to compensate for reductions on the 462 Leatherhead-Chertsey service.

This of course left the Leatherhead-Esher section unserved. The opportunity was taken to use an independent operator to provide a modest service of six buses a day on Mondays to Fridays only between these points, using a minibus. This became Mole Valley route 1, and was an example of the County Council using a lower-cost operator where that seemed a sensible option. This was a route which by then might have been termed marginal to the network as a whole.

The main thrust of the Council's policy though was the substitution of the very costly London Transport operations by those of London Country which, allowing for the earlier problems, had the resources so to do. A concomitant change was the withdrawal of financial support for the LT 265 route, then plying between Kingston and Leatherhead as successor to the 71 and 65 before it.

This would leave a substantial gap in the mile or so of the built-up northern end of Leatherhead to Woodbridge, as well as the links north. To provide a local service over this section and thence over the Greater London boundary at Malden Rushett, the 468 route was used. Thus the 468 was extended south from Chessington Zoo to Leatherhead. At the same time, it was extended at the other, Epsom, end of the route to serve Brettgrave, enabling the 419 Epsom town service to be withdrawn. This was a resource-based service revision and the route had a curious pigtail appearance on the map. It was created as it proved just possible to complete the Leatherhead-Brettgrave link within an hour, thus enabling an hourly frequency to be achieved with the use of only two vehicles.

The Village bus leaflet, which was launched on 27 November 1976, hence the seasonal wrapping. This was an attempt to provide a shopping service to a selection of villages, using a vehicle on three days a week which would otherwise be spare.
John Glover

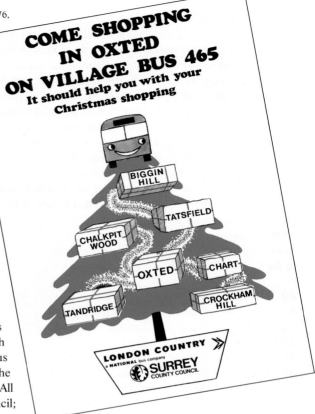

That left Green Line 714, an ailing route then running between Dorking and Victoria, and the opportunity was taken to change its nature. The original intention was for it to terminate at Kingston in the north and to be extended to Horsham in the south in lieu of the 414 which was withdrawn south of Dorking. In the event, a service to Victoria was maintained at two-hourly intervals, while that between Dorking and Kingston was on a 30/60 min headway. Not all services proceeded south of Dorking.

The revisions described, plus further changes affecting Dorking, took place on 31 August 1980. On deregulation, while the 408 and 714 survived as commercial services run by London Country South West (LCSW) and in a similar form, the 468 (minus Brettgrave) was tendered as 568, while what was the revised 416 had already been dismembered again. All formed parts of contracts let by the County Council; LCSW won the 562, which was rerouted from Leatherhead via Oxshott.

218 Kingston-Hersham-Walton-Shepperton-Staines
219 Kingston-Hersham-Weybridge
437 Guildford-West Byfleet-Weybridge

The 218 and 219 London Transport routes were amongst the busiest operated by that organisation in Surrey and, like others before them, were considered for transfer to London Country.

These routes ran as a combined service to Hersham, where they split. While the 218 to Staines was generally felt to be satisfactory as it was, the 219 terminated at what was then Weybridge BAC Works. There were various opportunities for its incorporation into other London Country routes in the Addlestone and Woking area, using an area scheme approach rather than just the one route. About 15% of the two routes together lay within Greater London, the boundary with Surrey being at the Dittons.

Early work produced rough calculations as follows:

London Transport routes 218/219; costs and revenues pa, 1978 prices

	London Transport £'000	London Country £'000
Estimated costs	543	454
Estimated revenues	369	369
Deficit	174	85

This time, however, the response from London Transport to the opening of negotiations was rather different. Essentially, they would match London Country's operating costs, so eliminating any price advantage. This would also avoid any complications with fares matters within Greater London.

That, of course, put a new complexion on the whole issue. The upshot was that the 218 was retained as a London Transport service, but the amalgamation potential with the 219 was such that the transfer on this went ahead. Fares and service conditions compatible with London Country were introduced on London Transport's 218 over the common section between Kingston and Hersham.

The 219 was extended through to Woking and was operated by London Country as a spine through the area. Seven other local routes were revised to provide a supporting role. This produced a financial saving and a more attractive network, which in itself brought in more revenue.

The 219 now operated as London Country 437 between Kingston and Woking, and was extended thence to Guildford. The half-hourly frequency was retained, as with the 218, as far as Weybridge. Alternate journeys terminated at Addlestone; others proceeded hourly to West Byfleet, Woking and Guildford. The transfer took place on 29 January 1983.

On deregulation, the 218 passed initially to London Country South West. The 437 was registered by LCSW as a commercial service on Mondays to Saturdays, and the company gained the Sunday service under contract to the County Council. It was however terminated at Woking.

80 Morden-Banstead Cross Roads-Lower Kingswood (Sundays)
80A Morden-Banstead Cross Roads-Walton on the Hill (Sundays)
164 Morden-Banstead-Epsom
164A Morden-Banstead-Tattenham Corner
280 Tooting-Banstead Cross Roads-Lower Kingswood (Mondays to Saturdays)
280A Tooting-Banstead Cross Roads-Walton on the Hill (Mondays to Saturdays)
711 Reigate-High Wycombe

Service reorganisation in the Banstead area went through a number of distinct stages. First, the 80/80A and 280/280A were reorganised to run via Banstead centre as opposed to just the rather distant Cross Roads, which enabled them to follow the direct route out of Sutton and traverse the length of the High Street.

It was proposed that they should then follow the road used by Green Line 711 to continue their route, though unfortunately the Traffic Commissioner ruled against its use in a four-day court case. This had the effect of requiring extra resources to cover the additional time taken.

Having regained their original route on the A217 Brighton Road, the Lower Kingswood buses proceeded as previously. However, the 80A/280A were diverted via Tattenham Way and Great Tattenhams to Merland Rise, thence via the 406 route to Tadworth station and continuing on their original route. This took the 80A/280A buses to more housing areas, and also enabled the 164A to Tattenham Corner, which they nearly reached, to be withdrawn.

The next event was the withdrawal of Green Line 711 by London Country in October 1977. This was precipitated by the termination of GLC support, and it was replaced at the southern end by a new bus service 422 running from Sutton, inside the Greater London boundary, to Reigate as before and on to Redhill.

The last development was the cessation of all London Transport services beyond Banstead High Street. The 164 to Epsom was terminated there, and the gap filled by a new London Country service, the 418 — not to be confused with the previous use of the number mentioned above. The 418 originated in Sutton, taking the same route as the superseded 164 to Epsom and was extended thence to Leatherhead.

The 422 service was enhanced to run daily instead of Mondays to Saturdays and extended beyond Redhill to Gatwick and Crawley, though not on Sundays. This, the final phase, was introduced on 24 April 1982.

The 420 and 422 were registered as commercial services by London Country South West from October 1986, which also won the tenders for the Sunday service. The 418 link survived in a different form, but was not registered. LCSW won the operation of the Sunday service. London Buses registered operation of the 164 to Banstead, but on Mondays to Saturdays only.

The weekend leisure facility was also pursued in Kent with the 418, seen here at a roadside stop on Bitchet Common. This was a 37-mile route, with passengers picked up and set down anywhere it was safe so to do. *Ian Allan Library*

211 Walton-on-Thames-Kingston-Tolworth

The 211 service was withdrawn on 29 January 1983, to be replaced by London Country's route 461 from St Peter's Hospital, Chertsey, through to Walton and terminating in Kingston, using the same routeing. In addition, Green Line 716 was diverted to serve Hurst Park.

The service changes outlined are only a selected portion of the large total that took place. Many, but not all, illustrate the gradual movement away from London Transport operation and replacement by that of London Country. While given the duty of co-ordination, Surrey County Council was invested with no additional powers so to do. Consequently, the Council had to rely solely on its ability to influence and persuade — mainly by fiscal means.

The Council attached considerable importance to the early establishment by the Public Transport Team of effective links with the operators and with the District Councils. They recognised on the one hand that transport management was primarily a matter for the operators and on the other that District Councils often had a more exact knowledge of the needs of their area. The experience and knowledge of both groups were, therefore, essential to the efficient and sensitive discharge of the Council's responsibilities.

Furthermore, discussions at both Member and Officer level were promoted with Parishes (directly or through their County Association), with voluntary organisations (directly or through the Surrey Voluntary Service Council), with the Traffic Commissioners, with the Transport Users' Consultative Committees, rail and bus user groups and the Greater London Council and adjoining County Councils.

DORKING

The changes have been huge, but there were also quieter areas. What follows is an analysis of the changes which took place on services from Dorking from the end of London Transport operation in 1969 until the last timetable before deregulation in 1986.

Number of journeys from Dorking, Mondays to Fridays, including any schooldays-only services, showing final destinations

Departures, Dorking to or via:	LT Country Bus & Coach 14 June 1969		London Country 12 May 1986		Notes
Leatherhead	470 Croydon	26	470 Leatherhead	2	
	712/3 Dunstable	21	714 Kingston	21	(1)
	714 Luton	16			
Reigate	414 Croydon	26	414 Croydon	25	
			773 Brighton	15	(2)
Newdigate	439 Newdigate	19	439 Newdigate	4	
Chart Downs	449 Chart Downs	15	449 Chart Downs	22	
Goodwyns	449 Goodwyns	12	414 Goodwyns	7	
			449 Goodwyns	30	
Capel	414 Horsham	20	414 Capel	4	
		18	714 Horsham	18	
Sutton*	412 Sutton	6	T22 Guildford	5	(3)
Guildford	425 Guildford	26	773 Guildford	12	(2)
Ranmore	412 Ranmore	6	T22 Ranmore	1	(3), (4)

Notes:
(1) of which in 1986, six extended to Victoria
(2) 773 operated jointly with Brighton & Hove
(3) T22 operated by Tillingbourne
(4) Fridays only in 1986.
*   Sutton refers to the village of Sutton, between Holmbury St Mary and Abinger Hammer

The table shows that on the whole service levels remained remarkably constant over the intervening years. Such a table cannot tell everything; some routes are rather less direct now. Thus most 414 services make a diversion via Strood Green, costing 8min per journey and short workings to Westcott and the diversions via Dorking station are not shown.

Notable is the reduction of services via Leatherhead, and the starting of a service to Brighton. Services to the Chart Downs and Goodwyns estates have both been made more frequent.

The true rural areas have fewer services as might be anticipated. Routes such as T22 were devised to serve many small settlements south of the A25, which made Dorking-Guildford throughout times uncompetitive with the 773.

London Country thus retained a large proportion of the total operation. This can be compared with the situation in East Grinstead where a stream of service revisions over the years resulted in a much lower level of service than had existed earlier. However, the Dorking table compares the situation when London Country was set up with the pre-deregulation service level, now 20 years ago.

In Hertfordshire the Lea Valley Leisure Bus was the 318, photographed here at Dobbs Weir on 1 June 1980, *en route* to Broxbourne. *Trevor Whelan*

BOUNDARIES

Boundaries are a fact of life, certainly in local government. Both County and District Councils are essentially inward-looking bodies, with elected members trying to do the best they can for their electorate. But their writ stops at the boundary; what happens beyond is, in many ways quite literally, somebody else's problem. The person on the other side might have rather different views on matters like priorities and budgets, anyway.

However, public transport is about the provision of links where people want to travel, and few of these take much cognisance of where the county boundaries have been placed. Neither do they have much regard to the transport implications. So it is up to local authority officers to come to the best accommodation they can with their opposite numbers in adjoining authorities, with a view to reaching an acceptable compromise to members on both sides.

In the case of Surrey, the boundary issue had not been resolved as was anticipated. A look at the Greater London boundary as it presently exists shows that the south-west side is pulled in rather closer to the centre of the capital than elsewhere. For many years, it was anticipated that at least the areas of Epsom & Ewell and Banstead would form part of Greater London, but this did not happen. In bus terms, this meant that roundly half the 61 London Transport Central Buses routes which crossed the boundary into what the GLC dubbed the 'out counties' at the time of the split with Country Buses and Green Line, had a Surrey destination. The effects of this will be considered later.

This section examines the situation in Surrey, Greater London and Hertfordshire, as far as London Country Bus Services were concerned, in 1972.

Table: LCBS bus mileage in Surrey, 1972

	Mileage	% total
Mileage totally within Surrey	6,865,555	65.7
Parts of routes shared with Greater London	1,596,562	15.3
Parts of routes shared with other counties	1,993,405	19.0
Total mileage	10,455,522	100.0

From this, the importance of Greater London can be seen. This is not perhaps surprising given that it included such important traffic objectives for London Country as Croydon, Kingston and Heathrow. These London Country routes were of course in addition to those operated by London Transport, giving large cross-boundary traffic volumes.

The situation in Hertfordshire was rather different, demonstrating that in many ways Hertfordshire is more self-contained in its bus transport provision:

Table: LCBS bus mileage in Hertfordshire, 1972

	Mileage	% total
Within Hertfordshire	12,807,268	86.2
Shared with Greater London	489,248	3.3
Shared with other counties	1,553,222	10.5
Total mileage	14,849,738	100.0

All these, however, were strictly bus operations, and did not include Green Line coaches, tables for which follow:

Table: Green Line in Surrey, 1972

	Mileage	% total
Within Surrey	2,008,558	16.2
Elsewhere, same routes	10,368,078	83.8
Total mileage	12,376,636	100.0

Table: Green Line in Hertfordshire, 1972

	Mileage	% total
Within Hertfordshire	2,005,718	24.7
Elsewhere, same routes	6,100,243	75.3
Total mileage	8,105,961	100.0

The London Country invasion of London Transport territory saw a green Leyland National on the 461 sharing Kingston bus station with a red Routemaster on the 65 and a red Leyland National on the 218 for Staines. *John Glover*

While London County bus mileage within Hertfordshire was approaching twice the levels within Surrey, that for Green Line was marginally lower. In both cases, though, the domestic mileage for each county is swamped by the interests of others. In the case of the Green Line routes running between Surrey and Hertfordshire via central London, the interests of the GLC based on vehicle mileage operated was roundly 45%. With radial routes of this type, which then formed a large majority of the services operated, the views of the Greater London Council would be crucial. Their willingness or otherwise to support them where necessary was bound to be a decisive factor in their future.

London Country in 1980/81

The company carried 102.6m passengers in 1980 by bus and a further 9.6m by Green Line, a total of 112.2m passenger journeys.

The following table shows where the revenue support for London Country came from in 1980. It should be stressed that this is not the whole of such expenditure of the County Councils, since they all had other operators to call on their funds and the relative extent of London Country's services in their areas varied.

Revenue support to LCBS, 1980

	£'000
Bedfordshire	19
Berkshire	101
Buckinghamshire	213
Essex	646
Greater London Council	1,090
Hertfordshire	2,563
Kent	476
Surrey	2,056
West Sussex	240
Total revenue support	7,404

This represented around 18% of the company's total income.

At that time (16 May 1981), staffing and assets of the company were as follows:

London Country staff, 1981

Drivers	2,038
Mechanical staffs	872
Clerical and others	431
Management and supervisory	446
Total staff employed	3,787

No staff were allocated solely to either bus or coach activity. They were totally interchangeable for efficient operation, but on average 420 of the above drivers were employed daily on Green Line.

Vehicle requirements

Buses, local services	826
Green Line scheduled services	157
Green Line private hire and excursions	51
Total vehicle requirement	1,034

In retrospect

How well did it all work? Over the years, the mileage of London Transport buses in Surrey reduced to 22% of its 1976 level. Some of this was due to service level economies as had to be practised everywhere, but the great majority was due to the transfer of services to London Country. There were other transfers, including from London Country to independents, but these were of considerably less overall significance.

In so doing, the Council needed to proceed with caution. Key questions were:

- Could the potential replacement operator do what he claimed to be able to do, either profitably or, if not, at a pre-determined and acceptable revenue support cost?
- As a body charged with the duty of providing services to meet the needs of the travelling public, what risks would the County Council be taking on the public's behalf?
- What reaction, if any, might be expected from the displaced operator, both in that vicinity and elsewhere in the County?

Happily, no insuperable problems were encountered, and the cumulative effect was that the Council benefited from savings of £1.5-£2million a year on their support costs, compared with the situation had the original operators continued.

The planned changes were accomplished with minimal disruption to travel patterns, but had nevertheless been achieved at times by vociferous and prolonged public reaction, despite consultation. An abiding memory is that of a lady who phoned up in protest about the cutting back of London Transport's 237 service from Chertsey to Lower Sunbury. After an inordinate time had been spent on an explanation of why it was happening and how the replacement LCBS service would operate, she eventually riposted with 'I am thinking you are an imbecile!' 'Quite right, too' was one's response, followed by a hasty replacement of the receiver. It was time to go for lunch.

Large-scale change of this nature is never easy, but that doesn't mean that it can't be, or shouldn't be, tackled.

Schools traffic near Tadworth could not always be accommodated on one Leyland National, but the driver here was successful in taking all the crowd. The photographer decided to wait. *John Glover*

7   **Green Line**

'Service, Comfort and Speed with Safety.'

Traffic notice to staff, issued shortly after the creation of Green Line Coaches Ltd, 1930

As already recounted briefly, the London General Omnibus Company formed an express department in 1928 and the following October started its first coach service between Watford and Golders Green, where it connected with the Underground. In January 1930 a second service linked Watford direct to Charing Cross, and services to Slough and Windsor followed quickly.

In conjunction with the independent East Surrey, 12 AEC Regal coaches were acquired, the 'T'-type, to run between Redhill, Reigate and Oxford Circus. Similar arrangements were made with National in the north.

By mid-1930, an integrated coach network was well advanced, and Green Line Coaches Ltd came into being on 9 July 1930. The first service under the Green Line name left Guildford for Charing Cross on 17 July 1930 and by October the following year the new company had 275 coaches on 27 different routes.

The expansion of Green Line operations did, however, attract police objections as a result of traffic

Eccleston Bridge sees several Green Line routes together, now equipped with 'proper' coaches, though in the background a Leyland National has sneaked in. It is 1980. *John Glover*

congestion. Several routes had already been linked across central London and an off-street coach station at Poland Street, near Oxford Circus, was opened in 1930. There was pressure to remove coaches from central London altogether, but it was eventually agreed that stops would be limited in the central zone and there would be no street parking of coaches within the zone. Thus Green Line's London operations became centred at (one might say almost monopolised) Eccleston Bridge, Victoria, slightly outside the zone.

The unification of London's public transport brought about by the creation of the LPTB in 1933 saw the independent operators who had also been providing coach services on a similar basis selling out, a process which was virtually completed by early 1934. This gave a new impetus to network development.

GREEN LINE AND LONDON COUNTRY

Green Line was developed in the 1930s and reinstated after World War 2. Its traditional limited-stop, cross-central-London coach network gathered more and more problems as time progressed. Due, perhaps, to traffic congestion in the main, the service became increasingly unreliable, passengers slowly abandoned it and profitability suffered.

Network pruning was carried out, but by 1975 Green Line's deficit totalled £1.6million. A decision had to be made by the company whether to withdraw what remained, or to invest in rebuilding it with a completely fresh image.

SERVICE PERFORMANCE

The sections that follow are based on a consultancy report for the company.

In 1973 the working expenses on operating Green Line amounted to about 19% of the total bus and coach operations combined. On a cost base of £2.7m, revenue amounted to £2.9m and this demonstrated a modest profit. But this was in a year of a rail strike, which inflated profits by around £50,000. Noticeable was the higher revenue during the summer months, with the four weeks ending 8 September 1973 the highest at £258,000 as against £184,000 in the four weeks ended 27 January.

The profit so claimed did not cover overhead costs. With these included, routes fell into three categories:

- those which showed a profit throughout the year (704, 705, 715, 715A, 716, 720, 721, 723, 725, 727)
- those subject to a seasonal variation, with a profit during the year but a loss during the winter (706, 708, 718)
- those not making a full contribution to overheads throughout the year (701, 711, 712, 713, 714, 716A, 719, 724). In mitigation, the 701, 714, 719 and 724 showed a profit during July and August.

By some margin, the busiest routes, in terms of passenger journeys, were the 721 and 725, with 35,000 and 32,000 passengers respectively in a sample week. Next was the 715/715A at a fraction under 20,000 and the 723 at 18,000.

Many individual changes were considered, one of which was the withdrawal of the last four journeys in each direction on the 708. The illuminating comment reads as follows. 'Because this route cannot efficiently be divided in Central London within the existing Union Agreement, an investigation was carried out to combine the operation of the East Grinstead-London section of route with the Bus OMO schedule at East Grinstead, to determine if this could provide a satisfactory formula for the withdrawal of evening journeys. The service between Hemel Hempstead and London could be operated within the existing Union Agreement without involving the bus schedule at Hemel Hempstead.'

A detailed calculation followed, concluding that the loss of receipts from the 'carry-over' traffic across Central London as well as that from the withdrawn journeys themselves would be £662 per week, but costs (crew, mileage, vehicle and administration) would increase by £274 per week. The conclusion was that 'this type of operation cannot be considered'.

Other proposals for the removal of evening journeys which had been performing less well produced a more successful prognosis, and were implemented.

NEW ROUTES?

What were the practical problems of terminating routes in central London? Without negotiations with the T&GWU, it appeared that the 712/713 (Dunstable-Dorking) were the only possibility. This gave rise to a scheme to reorganise these routes thus:

703 Dorking-Victoria-Baker Street
712 Victoria-Baker Street-Park Street-St Albans
713 Victoria-Baker Street-Shenley-St Albans

and this was done. If, after introduction, the overlap section was not successful, consideration might be given to withdrawing the 703 and instituting a new route from St Albans to Victoria, then via the M4 to Heathrow Airport and Windsor.

Another option considered was diverting the 701 west of Staines to operate to Windsor and covering the Staines-Ascot section by diverting the 718, to use spare capacity on 701 and relieve pressure on the 718 which served both Hampton Court and Windsor.

Although a saving in operating costs was achieved, this did result in the loss of one coach an hour between Hampton Court and Windsor which would cause inadequacy on the 725 over this section. There would also be no service direct from Ascot to the Staines to Hounslow section, while there would also be possible inadequacy between Hammersmith and Staines during the summer. In turn, this might lead to duplication being required on both the 701 and 718. It was therefore decided not to proceed; on such detailed considerations are such decisions taken.

Was there any future in extending Green Line services to reach new areas, beyond Green Line's present outer termini? Both the 701 (Ascot) and 719 (Wrotham) were considered in this context. The proposal was that the 701 should be extended to Bracknell and the 719 to Maidstone — 'somewheres, rather than nowheres'. For a start, this would mean more vehicles and more drivers, but of course there was the potential of extra revenue.

How likely was this? Problem number one was seen as the service offered by British Rail. Fast trains from Bracknell reached Waterloo in 44min, slow ones in 56min. The corresponding time by the 701 (to Victoria) would be around 100min, and this did not sound like good business. It would be possible to serve some West London destinations rather better than rail could, but even so the 701 was withdrawn in October 1975.

The reason for this gloomy outlook was that only 6% of passengers travelled more than 20 miles on the existing network. Bracknell was around 30 miles as were Stevenage and Hemel Hempstead. Traffic gains seemed likely to be minimal.

Much the same applied to Maidstone, where Maidstone & District already operated six journeys a day to Victoria on behalf of National Travel. There was also the additional complication in that the availability of the 719 between Swanley, Farningham, West Kingsdown and Wrotham had enabled the bus service to be largely withdrawn, with a considerable saving in bus operating costs.

OTHER IDEAS

Another idea was the combination of Green Line 724 with Eastern National's 151 and 251 to form a route linking Romford-Wanstead-Wood Green-Finchley-Edgware-Harrow-Uxbridge-Staines. The comparison was with the 725, which ran through and linked the important commercial centres of Gravesend, Dartford, Bromley, Croydon, Sutton and Kingston, and which also provided a service from all of these to Hampton Court and Windsor for pleasure traffic. Somehow, the fleshpots of Wanstead and Finchley were not in the same category. The area might be considerably more densely populated than the 724 route, but the latter did offer a valuable east-west link through Essex and Hertfordshire.

Was there scope for terminating some Green Line operations at interchanges with British Rail or the Underground, or at least making more use of such opportunities? These might provide passengers with a faster service to Central London and coach punctuality should be improved. However, a survey of Green Line

Now in NBC livery, Alexander-bodied AEC Swift SMA3 on the 726 takes on passengers in the middle of Windsor in June 1977. *Barry Le Jeune*

709 which passed Brixton station found that of 122 passenger arrivals from the south at Brixton, ten alighted and of these only five continued by Underground. In the return direction, of the six picked up, only one was from the Victoria Line.

What was timekeeping really like on Green Line at that period? A week's survey in Central London in April 1973 revealed what was happening.

Late running by Green Line coaches
Central London, Monday 2 April-Friday 6 April 1973

	No of coaches	mins late		
		up to 10	11-30	more than 30
Northbound	1,588	1,229	288	71
Southbound	1,347	971	281	95
Total	2,935	2,200	569	166
As %	100	75	19	6

The percentage of coaches arriving 0-10 mins late was very high. The remaining coaches were confined mainly to the morning and evening peaks. The latter hard core of late running was seen as the major cause of passenger traffic decline in peak periods.

GREATER LONDON COUNCIL

The future of Green Line operations was a matter which concerned all the County Councils. Such operations were an important part of the total network, but their utility did suffer from the operational problems which impinged seriously on their reliability. If there was a route, and there were many, with both bus and Green Line services, was it realistic to rely on just one of them in, say, the evenings? Did Green Line really just duplicate rail provision?

What was certain was that the future of individual Green Line routes was not something on which any County Council could make a decision. If Green Line needed revenue support, it needed this from each and

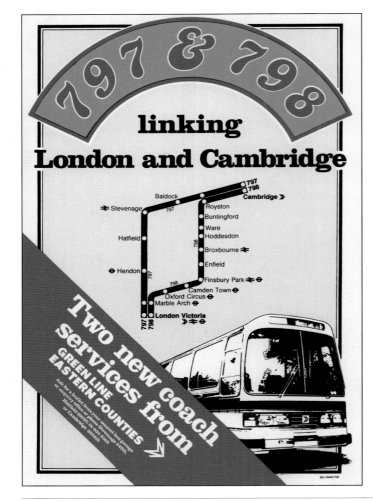

Left: A poster showing how far the Green Line network was now stretching, in conjunction this time with Eastern Counties. It is 1981. *Guy Brigden collection*

Above: The Green Line service on the 707/717 routes between Luton and Victoria was completely overhauled using new coaches from as early as 1977 as this timetable leaflet shows. *Author's collection*

every Council's area through which the route passed. The attitude of the Greater London Council was thus crucial to the outcome. How much support, if any, might the GLC feel able to offer for their part of the operation? Based on mileage operated, this might need to amount to around 50% of the total.

The response from the GLC was that, though Green Line traffic was relatively small, and declining, the primary function within Greater London was catering for different and more specialised types of traffic than ordinary bus routes. These included longer distance journeys, inter-suburban journeys and (with the 724/725/727) orbital journeys. Generally these were difficult journeys that could not be made by other bus or rail services.

Reliability was however seen as a problem, which was made worse by half-hourly or hourly service headways. This was considered to be a major factor undermining passenger confidence. The options for the future were seen as:

- Maintain the present policy of supporting individual services, with an annual review to justify retention on value for money terms
- Improve services on existing networks, by substantially increasing service frequencies, but this would have to be a selective policy due to its cost and the fact that it would also have implications for the County Councils. The orbital routes might be more easily justified

- Terminate Green Line services at suburban railheads, eg Golders Green, Turnpike Lane, Morden, Lewisham, etc. This would mean more passengers being required to change, which might negate one of the reasons they were using Green Line in the first place. Any services which terminated at an outer London railhead were unlikely to justify a GLC contribution to their retention
- Reroute radial services to cater for orbital movements in Greater London. This might stimulate demand, albeit only low frequency services would be offered. Two suggestions were made — reroute the 706/708 away from Victoria/Marble Arch to run from Croydon via Mitcham, Wimbledon, Putney and Hammersmith to Kilburn, and similarly with the 716 from Hammersmith to run via Kilburn, Brent Cross, Hendon and Finchley to Barnet instead of via Marble Arch.

There were also options for fares and conditions to come more into line with those then being espoused by the GLC for London Transport services.

One suburban terminal then being canvassed was for the northern part of the 718 Harlow-Victoria-Windsor, which might be truncated at Walthamstow Central station, where both Underground and British Rail could be accessed. Like the GLC, the County Councils did agree that the three orbital services were likely to be worth supporting in broadly their existing form, at least for the time being. As always, there were different approaches by different Councils; the representative from West Sussex declared that his Council was unlikely to pay for anything they could avoid.

THE 1976 REVIEW

The above was largely by way of preliminaries. There were clearly large-scale problems which were encompassed in the Green Line Network Review.

The aim was to achieve viability on each route. The total effect of the proposals was to replace the estimated deficit of £467,000 a year, before fixed costs were charged, by an estimated contribution towards fixed costs of £85,000. The overall deficit set against total costs (before revenue support) fell from £1.298million to £746,000, of which it was anticipated that more than £500,000 could reasonably be expected from revenue support in a notional year. Indeed it could, as events later showed.

The proposals were as follows:

700 new service London Victoria-Windsor, Express via M4

A summer-only service operating daily, every hour, was proposed to run non-stop via the M4 to fulfil the following purposes:

- To carry the heavy traffic levels, particularly tourists, more efficiently than the stopping services between central London and Windsor
- To attract shopping and possibly commuter traffic from Windsor, which was said to have an unattractive rail service
- To compensate during the summer months for the withdrawal of the 718 between London and Windsor (it actually survived)
- To create capacity on the parallel stopping service 704 to cater for the Heathrow Airport traffic generated by its diversion via Heathrow
- The traffic carried during the first summer of operation would need to be monitored with a view to considering the justification for winter operation, without which the prospect of building commuter traffic diminished. This is what happened
- Special fares appropriate for the tourist market would be charged.

703 Dorking-Epsom-London

Service withdrawn 2 October 1976, with some transfer of revenue to the 714 on the Dorking-Leatherhead section. There was no GLC support.

704 Windsor-London-Sevenoaks-Tunbridge Wells

The nearest stop to Heathrow Airport on the 704 was on Bath Road at Heathrow North. It was proposed to divert this route via Heathrow Airport (Central) thus providing a direct link to the Airport from Windsor, Central London, South East London and Kent. It was considered that the 704 should be diverted via the Colnbrook bypass to provide a more direct and attractive service. This would also help compensate for the additional time taken in accessing Heathrow.

No additional coaches were needed, but there were some additional crew costs. The diversion was implemented in May 1977.

705 Windsor-London-Westerham-Sevenoaks

It was felt that there was potential in providing a direct fast link from the Biggin Hill areas towards Bromley and London, for which the following measures were proposed:

- Reroute the 705 at Keston via a direct route in lieu of a circuitous route via Keston 'Mark'
- Equate 705 fares from Biggin Hill to Bromley with parallel bus fares to remove disincentive to coach travel, relieve pressure on route 410 and utilise spare capacity on route 705
- Carry out a marketing exercise in the Biggin Hill area, based on the faster service on the 705 with more attractive fares.

It was also thought that further journeys should be rerouted to operate a spur from Westerham to Chartwell on summer Sundays, at no duty or vehicle cost. That would be in lieu of the extension of route 706 journeys from Chelsham, the latter route having been withdrawn by summer 1977.

The 705 was also diverted into Heathrow, as with the 704.

706 Chelsham-Croydon-London-Watford-Aylesbury
708 East Grinstead-Croydon-London-Watford-Hemel Hempstead

These routes were to be combined from April 1977 into an hourly East Grinstead-Aylesbury service via Hemel Hempstead. It was also proposed to examine parallel bus operations between Watford and Aylesbury, and between Godstone and East Grinstead to avoid unnecessary duplication of facilities and improve Green Line receipts. Neither route was supported by the GLC.

707 New semi-express service, Luton Airport-London Victoria

A new semi-express route was proposed to operate every day, hourly between morning and early evening, observing the majority of existing 714 stops between Luton and St Albans, and then only at major points between St Albans and London. To minimise running time, the basic service would operate via Barnet, Finchley, Golders Green and Marble Arch. Certain journeys would be diverted between London Colney and Golders Green to serve Brent Cross, thus providing the shopping centre with a link from places such as Luton and Berkhamsted.

The following functions were seen:

- To test the principle of semi-express operation on Green Line which, if successful, could be extended to other Green Line routes
- To replace partially and retain all possible traffic on routes 712/713/714 which were proposed for withdrawal in their present form
- To serve the Brent Cross shopping centre for which there was potential demand from Hertfordshire towns
- To provide a regular service between Central/North London and Luton Airport, which was not served by the 714.

No allowance was made for revenue support for this route.

Green Line was also running seaside excursions; this one to Brighton, using a Leyland Olympian, was photographed at Caterham, Tally Ho! on 18 May 1985. It ran as the 709, now long deceased on a daily basis. *Guy Brigden*

709 Godstone-Baker Street

This route was converted to one-man operation and reduced from three coaches to two from 15 May 1976. Finally, it was running two morning and two evening rush hour journeys in each direction Monday-Friday and two on Sundays. No further savings were possible, short of complete withdrawal. If the latter were contemplated, full revenue support should first be sought. This was not forthcoming and the service was withdrawn on 27 October 1979.

711 Reigate-London-High Wycombe

The northern section of the 711 operated parallel to Oxford South Midland's express service 290 and it was intended to rationalise the two as a joint exercise. This could result in a separation of the northern section, with semi-express operation via Western Avenue between Uxbridge and London.

At the time, the Reigate-Sutton section was under discussion with Surrey County Council with a view to taking over certain London Transport bus traffic, so a decision on withdrawal was deferred until this was resolved. The GLC declined to support the 711.

712/713 St Albans-Borehamwood-Golders Green-London
714 Luton-St Albans-Barnet-London-Kingston-Dorking

The original 712/713 cross-London services were terminated at Victoria from the north on 31 May 1975, which also saw the introduction of the 703 Dorking-Baker Street. The withdrawal of all these routes, with the exception of the Dorking-London section of the 714, was planned for 29 January 1977. They would be partially replaced in the north by new route 707.

The southern section of the 714 received revenue support both from the GLC and Surrey County Council and it could benefit from reductions in the 716/716A and the proposals for the 718.

Such had been the expansion of Green Line traffic that five Leyland Olympian coaches with 72-seat ECW bodies were introduced on the 720 service to Dartford and Gravesend. They were based at Northfleet, and the date is 4 June 1984. This is LRC4. *John Glover*

715/715A Hertford-London-Kingston-Guildford

In order to serve the important commercial and shopping centre of Kingston, it was proposed that route 715 be diverted via Hampton Court and Kingston in lieu of the Kingston bypass, to run as 715A on Saturdays. This service would then lend itself to replacing LT 215 between Cobham and Esher, after rerouting in Cobham. Any additional peak journeys needed would be supported financially by Surrey County Council.

Given the number of coaches then operating at peak periods between Guildford and Kingston, it would be possible to introduce semi-express operation between Guildford and London to attract commuters and other regular traffic.

In order to provide a common routeing in and out of London for the three routes serving Kingston (714/715/716), it was proposed to reroute the 715 via Kensington and Hyde Park Corner instead of Shepherd's Bush. This would have the advantage of serving the popular shopping area of Kensington.

716 Woking-London-Stevenage-Hitchin

This route was reduced from two to one coach an hour from 15 May 1976. The improved reliability resulted in the restoration of passenger confidence. It was concluded that time should be allowed to build further on this before contemplating further changes. There was no GLC support.

The service from the south was terminated at Oxford Circus on 28 January 1978.

717/718 Bishop's Stortford-Harlow-Epping-GLC railhead

These two new routes were planned to be introduced in consultation with Essex and Hertfordshire County Councils. The existing 718 and 720 routes, neither of which were supported, would be withdrawn.

The Walthamstow bus station terminal for new route 718 was agreed with London Transport. The bus station serves the Victoria Line station and the route provided an ideal opportunity to introduce an experimental through road/rail ticket. The terminal for the 717 was as yet undetermined.

It was felt that one of these routes could subsequently be the nucleus of a northern orbital route, similar in concept to the 725. The two routes would provide a joint 30min service over the common section of route (Epping-Bishop's Stortford). This would enable parallel bus services 396/397, 812 to be withdrawn.

A small deficit would result, but the routes would be likely to attract revenue support from both Essex and Hertfordshire if necessary.

718 Harlow-London-Hampton Court-Windsor
720 Bishop's Stortford-Harlow-London Aldgate

It was proposed that both routes be withdrawn in their then form, with various replacements as listed elsewhere. There was no GLC support, but the London-Windsor portion of the 718 was subsequently treated as commercial.

719 Hemel Hempstead-Garston-London-Swanley-Wrotham

The village of Wrotham, Kent, was too minor a traffic objective to be satisfactory. The proposal was to extend the route to Maidstone via the A20, thus enabling National Travel to operate its express service via the M20. This would cost one additional vehicle and six extra drivers at Swanley (on the basis that the entire service was extended). However, the financial equation was not yet satisfactory.

The northern end of the 719 paralleled bus 347/347A on the Watford-Hemel Hempstead section, but it was felt that revenue on 719 must increase with the rationalisation of services 706/708. Both schemes were being discussed with the County Councils concerned; the route was split in Central London on 27 October 1979.

721 Brentwood-Romford-London Aldgate

The level of service was to be reduced by one half from 2 October 1975. Attempts were also being made to agree a more competitive fares policy with London Transport for the section between Romford and London. If both these measures failed to achieve route viability, the route would be completely withdrawn with the resultant closure of Romford garage.

724 Romford-St Albans-Heathrow Airport-Staines

The section of route between Romford Market and Romford station was relatively poorly used and it was felt that the time taken to cover this small section, which was particularly prone to traffic delay, could be better used to extend the route beyond the unsatisfactory terminal at Staines garage to the real traffic objective, which was Staines town centre. No additional costs were involved.

In addition, a further extension of the route to Windsor would be made practicable in the event of the closure of Romford garage, when it would be necessary to transfer the operation to Harlow. At the same time it would then be possible to transfer the Staines operation to Windsor, thereby facilitating the closure of Staines. The additional costs involved would be the additional coach and eight additional drivers.

The Windsor service began on 2 April 1977.

This Leyland Tiger/Duple Dominant IV coach, TD5, was new in 1983. It is seen here at Oxford, Cornmarket/Queen Street on the 790 to Heathrow on 20 July 1985. *Guy Brigden*

Leyland Nationals were ousted from Green Line duties by influxes of new coaches. This is coach-seated SNC163 in Pimlico on the short-lived 703 Dorking service after it had been split in central London. It is 26 September 1976. *Guy Brigden*

726 Gravesend-Dartford-Bromley-Croydon-Kingston-Heathrow Airport-Windsor

The traffic carried to Heathrow Airport by routes 724 and 727 indicated the desirability of providing improved links to the Airport from other large areas of population without a direct facility. By diverting alternate journeys on the 725 via Heathrow instead of Staines and renumbered 726, links would be provided from large residential and commercial centres in South London to Heathrow. This was thought likely to generate considerable additional revenue at little cost.

The 726 routing from Kingston would be via Hampton Court, Hatton Cross and Heathrow Airport (Central) and the M4. No additional coaches were needed, nor any additional duties on weekdays. However, on Sundays, in order to provide one coach an hour on the 726 throughout the traffic day in addition to one coach an hour on the 725 overall increases were needed.

The new service began on 7 May 1977.

727 Crawley-Gatwick Airport-Heathrow Airport-Luton Airport

In order to prevent both seasonal inadequacies and overloading, but also to offer a more attractive service to connect with flights at both Heathrow and Gatwick, summer augmentation to two coaches an hour over the southern section between Crawley and Heathrow was felt most necessary. It was introduced in summer 1977.

728 Dunstable (Houghton Regis)-London via M1

Investigations were carried out into the viability of an express service via the M1, forming a commuter coach link between Dunstable and London. Dunstable has no rail service, commuters making their way by United Counties bus or private car to Luton station. The Dunstable population of around 30,000 has a GLC overspill area at Houghton Regis, and it therefore appeared a promising location for a commuter coach.

734 Addlestone-Heathrow-Golders Green-Wood Green-Hertford
735 Oxford Circus-Wood Green-Hertford

The inter-urban hourly 734 limited-stop using four RB coaches from each of Addlestone and Hertford garages was introduced on 27 October 1979. It was designed by LCBS/LT/GLC to provide links through the western/northern suburbs of London. The timetable was devised to produce an average speed of 17mph throughout the GLC area, the speed attained by other conventional routes through this type of operating area. Northwards from Wood Green, it ran on the alternate half hour with the 735. This was one of the last two Green Line routes to be split in central London, the replacement for the northern section of the 715.

In practice, the average speed of the 734 worked out at $14^{1}/_{2}$ mph throughout the day, with off-peak journeys faring little better than those in the peak. This represented an average loss of 21min on journeys of 98min through the GLC area at a speed only marginally better than the average LCBS bus and correspondingly unattractive for medium- to long-distance passengers, both for length of journey and timekeeping.

Usage was such as to prompt its withdrawal as a main orbital route in less than 18 months. It was then to become an hourly off-peak shopping service between Hertford and Brent Cross on Mondays to Saturdays only, the western end having disappeared. This did limit the route's exposure to some of the worst congestion points, though it was still left with the Palmers Green-Wood Green-Turnpike Lane section and Golders Green. A turnround time of 11min was allowed at Brent Cross.

747 Jetlink Gatwick-Heathrow

This hourly non-stop inter-airport service was introduced in April 1979, with a journey time of 70min, and was accelerated when it moved to the M23/M25 as the latter was completed during the 1980s.

After the M25 opened through in October 1985 a luxury Speedlink service was also started between Heathrow and Gatwick only, running every 20min using luxury high-floor 37-seat Leyland Tiger/Berkhof vehicles in a special Ray Stenning yellow, blue and red livery, based on NBC's standard coach style, and check-in desks at each terminal. Speedlink replaced the British Caledonian helicopter link between the airports, which was discontinued the following February, ostensibly for environmental reasons, although the helicopter service, which had started in 1978, was always intended to end when the M25 was opened throughout. Speedlink's scheduled journey time was just 50min.

Four new Leyland Tiger/Berkhof coaches lined up on the tarmac at Gatwick Airport, representing the four types of service on which they would run. From left to right these were Private Hire, National Express, Jetlink (Gatwick to Heathrow) and Flightline (Gatwick to London). *Ian Allan Library*

Victoria Coach Station on 4 June 1984 sees Flightline 777 as a service operated jointly by Green Line and Southdown. The service was non-stop to Gatwick in 70mins with (then) a fare of £2. These Plaxton-bodied Leyland Leopards are both Southdown vehicles. *John Glover*

Jetlink was revamped at the same time with new coaches, also mainly BTL-class Tiger/Berkhofs, and improved to half-hourly. The service was extended to run on alternate hours to Watford Junction station, Hemel Hempstead bus station, Luton station and Luton Airport. On the other hours it ran to the two Luton stops first and then continued to Stevenage station and then the bus station. Other journeys terminated at Heathrow.

It was an interesting exercise in market segmentation. Speedlink offered greater luxury, with tables and on-board toilets, a higher frequency and better check-in facilities for a £9 single fare, while Jetlink, though still with new coaches, offered a more basic service at half the price. Both were considerably cheaper than the helicopter, which cost £24 single by 1985.

750 Gravesend-Bromley-Purley-Gatwick-Crawley
This short-lived service was introduced in 1980 as an experiment at the request of the GLC and Kent County Council.

FARES AND TICKETING
Green Line fares were on a conventional mileage scale across the whole system, with singles, off-peak day and weekend returns and season tickets generally available on all services. Many routes had an element of special fares on sections where parallel bus facilities had been withdrawn, or reduced to run at certain times only. This resulted in exceedingly complicated faretables which were not readily understood.

With the 724 and 727 (only), the principle of selectively pricing journeys which started and/or finished at airports had been introduced. It was now proposed to examine, route by route, the comparative fares position with other modes and to introduce individually compiled faretables designed to maximise revenue and passenger appeal. Efforts would also be made to produce fares tables which were marketable and readily understood by staff and public alike. This might include limiting the number of fare stages. In cases where Green Line was expected to fulfil an existing or new local bus service need, co-ordination of bus and Green Line fares would be complete.

It was considered that the general policy of offering concessions at off-peak times only for return travel and for children was appropriate and should not be altered. A more acceptable way of selling season tickets was needed, especially where the company had no office in the vicinity.

A primary problem was the control exerted by London Transport on fares and conditions, but this could not be allowed to produce the sort of complicated, anomalous and confusing fares structures that would otherwise result.

Combined road/rail ticketing was considered to be a practical proposition, but only where the combined facility did not compete with an existing directly provided facility. Interchange is always a mixed blessing, and a direct service was likely to be preferred by the passenger if it were available. Besides, what operator would wish to share revenue if there was a chance of retaining it all for himself? Another problem in this area was vastly different fare policies, notably those of British Rail.

EVALUATION

The table below gives the anticipated results of such widespread change. V/SV represents the variable and semi-variable costs, explained earlier, and the margin is the extent to which these are covered by revenue. This still leaves the fixed costs, which in this group were estimated at £831,000, towards which the surplus of £85,000 made a useful contribution but still with another £746,000 to be covered. However, more than £500,000 might reasonably be expected in the notional year, so the routes concerned were coming very close to meeting all their allocated costs.

The PVR is the peak vehicle requirement, the main resource measurement in terms of the number of coaches which need to be employed at the peak to cover the requirements of the timetable.

**Green Line services exercise 1976
figures for a notional year**

Route	estimated revenue £'000	V/SV costs £'000	margin £'000	vehicle miles	PVR
700	36	25	11	77,000	1.5
704	363	337	26	877,548	9.0
705	198	226	-28	576,394	7.1
706/8	362	297	65	939,744	10.3
707	128	126	2	309,400	4.0
709	24	24	0	54,964	2.0
711	203	238	-36	670,904	8.4
714	103	114	-11	322,650	3.5
715/A	368	380	-12	1,135,368	14.7
716	313	333	-20	891,332	9.0
717/8	222	184	38	591,136	6.0
719	265	330	-65	826,695	7.7
723	261	250	11	625,352	10.0
724Ex	244	240	3	885,248	7.5
725/6	478	455	22	1,324,668	16.6
727Ex	416	336	79	1,127,464	12.0
728	11	11	0	42,130	1.0
Total	3,993	3,908	85	11,277,998	130.3

The discussion above is by no means a comprehensive list of Green Line services operated; rather it is an indication of the findings of those who studied the very real problems of Green Line in the 1970s, their conclusions, and actions taken.

TRANSPORT ACT 1980

The Transport Act 1980 deregulated express coaches, which made it much easier for Green Line to extend its routes to serve places like Oxford, Cambridge and the South Coast. It also formed alliances with other bus companies to operate routes jointly. Notable amongst these were Southdown, Alder Valley, Oxford South Midland, United Counties and Eastern Counties. The same Green Line name was used to market travel sales activities.

FLEET

A sight which was to become synonymous with Green Line appeared in 1952, the RF coach. The RF used a sleek, modern body design and an updated, underfloor version of the same AEC engine which had powered the T-types of the 1930s. Over 300 were built to replace a hotchpotch of old, unserviceable or hired vehicles that was Green Line's legacy after the war, and they were to be the mainstay of the network for more than 20 years. Even after withdrawal from coach use, such was the RF's durability that the last examples survived in bus service until 1979.

The fleet inherited from London Transport in 1970 had a number of vehicles for coaching use which might at a pinch have still included the elderly RFs. More usefully, the builds of Routemasters to coach specifications with higher seating specifications, luggage racks and platform doors, both the short (RMC) and long (RCL) varieties were fine — apart from their inability to be single manned. Only the small fleet of 14 AEC Reliances (RC) built for Green Line work in 1965 perhaps really counted, and they were not the most reliable of vehicles.

Following London Country's acquisition of 90 Park Royal-bodied AEC Reliances (RP) in 1971-72, they quickly found themselves on many Green Line routes; these were not very likeable vehicles though they lasted until 1985. Most had by this time been downgraded to bus work.

The new brooms though decided to acquire large fleets of real coaches with the appropriate bodywork. Apart from five (P) which arrived in 1973, a total of 150 were delivered between 1977 and 1979 (RS, RB). These were again AEC Reliances, with 'proper' coach bodies by Plaxton (RS) and Duple (RB), and were leased on a five-year basis which would thus give them a limited and pre-determined lifespan with their operator. Green Line routes were recast in 1977, to take account of the new coaches, which replaced buses with coach seats.

During the 1980s in the period up to deregulation and privatisation, Leylands started to appear. These consisted of 32 Leyland Leopards (DL, PL), followed by no fewer than 182 Leyland Tigers (TL, TD, TP, TPL). Then the first new double-deckers for Green Line for 20 years were 15 Leyland Olympians (LRC) and there were 85 more Leyland Tigers (BTL, STL, TDL) with high-floor coach bodies. The most unusual of these were the 53 BTLs, which had bodywork by Dutch builder Berkhof, previously very little-known in the UK; London Country's order, the first on Leyland Tiger chassis, is generally considered to have given Berkhof credibility in the UK market. The STLs were Plaxton-bodied and used the 'S' prefix to continue the tradition of the Plaxton-bodied RSs, whereby S stood for Scarborough, where Plaxton was based. Given the fame of the prewar STL double-decker on both Central and Country operations, they were no doubt so numbered by someone with a sense of history, humour or both. There were also a couple of Volvo B58s (DV) acquired for evaluation in 1980.

The coaches sported white livery with a wide green waistband and the name Green Line displayed prominently. They also, of course, carried the NBC symbol.

THE MARKET

Much of the above is included to show how thoughts on the future of Green Line were developing in the 1970s; not all the plans came about as anticipated. But they show how wide-ranging the thoughts were.

By 1982, London Country summed up Green Line as follows:

- All cross-London routes were split to improve reliability
- Universal use of new luxury standard coaches
- Expansion in the commuter and airport businesses
- More routes, reaching further afield, than at any time in its history
- Better-used traditional services between suburban towns and London retained, though often speeded up and generally improved
- Tourist services taking London visitors to destinations such as Windsor, Woburn Abbey and Chartwell
- Shopping excursions such as Hatfield to Milton Keynes, Harlow to Brent Cross, Dorking to Brighton
- Contributions to the National Express network

Left: The Leyland Olympian coaches were expanded to a fleet of 15. This promotional shot is presumably meant to demonstrate the nice places to which Green Line will take you, given half a chance. *Ian Allan Library*

Below: AN11 in Trafalgar Square on 14 April 1984; London Crusader was a marketing wing of London Country. *Guy Brigden*

- Contract services, from schools transport for the County Councils to staff movements for large concerns and the Round London Sightseeing Tour
- Private hire
- Excursions to anything from continental hypermarkets to three-day holiday breaks.

Somehow, the RF or RMC bus or coach doesn't seem quite right for these sorts of markets, but the old ones had gone. It took a long time for this to sink in fully.

Pleasingly, by the 1978/79 year, financial results were considerably better than anticipated in the 1976 review, partly due to the success of the 'commercial' routes and partly to the revenue support from the County Councils. Perhaps one might suggest that the network had by then been properly designed, rather than being the slightly tired remains of postwar recovery?

8 Deregulation and disposal

'The bus industry will be set free to give a better service to the passenger at less cost to the ratepayer and taxpayer.'

White Paper 'Buses', 1984

And so to the final stage of London Country's existence. Corporate planning was all the rage in the 1980s, and the following is taken from the company's plan for 1983/84. After this, of course, the forthcoming privatisation and deregulation loomed large.

COMPANY OBJECTIVES

The overall objective was to secure efficiently within the financial and statutory framework and having regard to the needs of the business for the longer term:

1. Local bus services and facilities which promote maximum patronage of such services by revenue-earning passengers, and
2. Coaching and other related services, facilities and supplies as may be provided under the company's statutory powers so as to make a commercial return on the investment.

There were also a number of supporting objectives, as follows. They are shown in full here as they indirectly offer a good view of the situation in London Country and also perhaps the bus industry as a whole in the early 1980s.

- To provide passenger transport services on the basis that, taking one year with another, total revenues exceed total charges properly chargeable against those revenues by £250k by the end of the Plan period (ie by 1986)
- Within the constraints imposed on the company, to maximise the provision of a planned, co-ordinated and efficient network of passenger transport services commensurate with the public requirements for such services in each local transport area
- To provide transport services meeting identified demands of the customer and their social needs, where the cost of such social provision is covered by Section 1 (of the Transport Act 1978) Revenue Support grants
- To maximise reliability of operation, which is fundamental to obtaining public confidence and thus retaining traffic, by improvement in engineering facilities and equipment, pursuance of strict maintenance control and establishment through local authorities of bus priority measures and traffic management schemes
- Reflecting on the effect of relaxed licensing laws, to improve operational efficiency of the company through effective use of manpower and capital assets and within the constraints imposed by the normal commercial disciplines, initiate change and be swiftly responsive to secure market share
- To continue to develop a close working relationship with County Councils and to assist them in conjunction with other public transport operators to carry out their transportation responsibilities under appropriate legislation

A G8 service from Guildford to Bushy Hill Estate operated by Guildford Leyland Atlantean AN22 on 4 January 1986. The livery now applied was bereft of any reference to NBC, a sign of the times. *Guy Brigden*

- To provide a positive image for the company through efficient operational performance and improved communication to customers, local authorities, the media and staff, such that the company becomes more integrated with the environment in which it operates
- To recognise the importance of manpower planning in the environment of changing operational requirements by development of company staff, staff replacement programmes, particularly supervisory and management levels, together with training and development of staff
- To promote employee participation in the wellbeing of the company and generally to enhance the working conditions and security of employment for its employees
- To perpetuate profitably the development of non-stage activities
- To plan a realistic level of investment in the company without which its objectives will not be capable of achievement.

LONDON COUNTRY IN 1983

During 1982 it was forecast that the mix of products would be as follows:

	% mileage	% income
Local buses, stage-carriage	69%	76%
Green Line, stage-carriage	28%	20%
National Express, excursions, private hire	3%	4%
Total	100%	100%

Thus the local bus services provided what the company called 'the bedrock of the operation'. By now the company had become inured to the consistent decline in this market; it was a fact of life. Over the three-year plan period from 1983 to 1986, passenger demand was forecast to decline by 2.5% pa if no other action was taken. But somebody else had other ideas about the future.

DEREGULATION

It was the view of the Conservative Government now in power that there was no case for retaining the bus industry in public ownership. It also took the view that the restrictive conditions (as they saw it) of the Road Service Licensing procedures should be abolished.

Their proposals were set out in the White Paper 'Buses', published in July 1984. What became the Transport Act 1985 provided as follows as far as London Country and the County Councils within its area were concerned. The three most important provisions in the present context were, in White Paper language:

- Bus services will be freed from restriction on competition by abolishing road service licensing throughout Great Britain, except for the framework of controls in London
- Many essential bus routes are not and never will be viable and local authorities will be able to continue to subsidise services that would cease in the free market. But they will be required to seek competitive tenders for contracts to run bus services which they wish to subsidise
- The structure of the bus industry must be allowed to change to meet market needs. The National Bus Company will be reorganised into smaller free-standing parts which will then be transferred to the private sector. All companies will compete with other operators for passengers and for contracts to run subsidised services.

Other elements were:

- Supervision of the quality and safety standards of public service vehicles and operators will be maintained and tightened
- Concessionary fares schemes will continue and all operators will be enabled to participate in them on an equitable basis
- The Government is determined to foster public transport in rural areas. Additional resources will be made available. Wider use of services run by education, health and social services authorities, the Post Office and others will be explored.

That was the summary of the proposals in the White Paper, which in the event passed into law with only minor amendment.

COMPANY REORGANISATION

A major part of the proposal was that the NBC subsidiaries should be sold to the private sector; initially, it was assumed, each as an integral unit. That was however not to be; companies such as London Country were far too large. The result was that this and three other companies were to be restructured. The concept of the smaller company was based on the premise that bus markets are relatively small and that small autonomous units will respond better to both the passenger and labour market than the unit which is part of the larger organisation.

However, certain specialised skills such as heavy engineering, secretarial, some accountancy, legal sales promotions and techniques and the purchasing of stores do benefit from scale. The plan was to bridge the gap by establishing operating companies which would be appropriate to the customer and labour markets and at the same time create autonomous service units or companies which would be appropriate to the benefits of scale and link the two by freely negotiated contracts.

On 13 February 1986, the Secretary of State issued a directive to the NBC to break up London Country Buses (and three other NBC subsidiaries: United Automobile, Crosville and Ribble) into smaller units by not later than 1 September 1986. Other companies had also been divided, including Southdown, United Counties, Bristol, Western National, Eastern National, Eastern Counties and Hants & Dorset.

Crawley's AN155 was a single door version of the build, seen here in Haslett Avenue on the C5 service to Ifield. It is 17 September 1983. *Guy Brigden*

It might be mentioned here that the main thrust of what became the Transport Act 1985, the deregulation of bus services, became fully operational on 26 October 1986 (deregulation day). It was not the best of times in which to conduct major structural reorganisation and dismemberment of the company!

LCBS SPLIT

And so it came about. Before deregulation, LCBS was split into four companies on a regional basis:

- London Country Bus (North East) Ltd. Traffic vehicles 352, 27% of traffic revenues
- London Country Bus (North West) Ltd. Traffic vehicles 318, 25% of traffic revenues
- London Country Bus (South West) Ltd. Traffic vehicles 397, 32% of traffic revenues
- London Country Bus (South East) Ltd, soon renamed Kentish Bus & Coach Co Ltd. Traffic vehicles 222, 16% of traffic revenues

This comparison shows that while LC(NE) and LC(NW) each fairly represented around a quarter of the total business, LC(SW) accounted for a third and Kentish Bus for only a sixth.

Further companies were created to look after London Country's central engineering works at Tinsley Green near Crawley (Gatwick Engineering Ltd) and to provide a joint marketing organisation for the Green Line name. This latter, Green Line Travel Ltd, was to be owned jointly by the four operating companies.

The restructuring of its subsidiary companies was to make them financially independent of the parent company, and of each other, as a prelude to their disposal to the private sector. The disposal programme confirmed the Government's wish that each of the subsidiaries should be sold separately, with limited exceptions. The main principles were the promotion of competition by selling the companies individually, offering employees an opportunity to acquire a controlling interest, giving regard to proposals for employee participation in bids from third parties, and the aim of completing as many bids as possible before deregulation day.

DEREGULATION MECHANICS

Each bus company, and that would include coach operators or others from outside the industry who had decided to obtain the necessary licences to operate, were obliged first to register the services they intended to provide from deregulation day. Registration (for a fee) would be with the Traffic Commissioner, but copied to the relevant County Council(s). The services registered had to include a timetable and details of the roads used, stopping places, etc.

It was the free choice of the operators to register services as they thought fit, but on the important condition that such operations would be commercial in nature and that no resort could be made to public funds if the venture proved less successful than anticipated. The Traffic Commissioner had to accept the registration formally, but was able to use reserve powers to refuse to accept it for safety or traffic congestion reasons. The County Councils were to have no say in what was, or was not, registered by the operators.

Conditions attached to such registrations were, in effect, that they should participate in any concessionary fare schemes for children or the elderly which the Council might operate, for which they would be reimbursed on a basis that saw them no better and no worse off than they would have been had they not been participating.

The registered services had to remain unchanged for the initial settling-in period, following which they could be altered or withdrawn at will by the operator, subject to giving 42 days' notice of any such intentions. Again, all such action was copied to the County Council(s).

Thus was established the basic network, which County Councils

This poster was displayed on bus shelters throughout Surrey, as an indication of what would shortly be happening on 26 October 1986. *John Glover*

London Buses launched its 306 between Epsom and Kingston at deregulation using Leyland Nationals, while London Country South West's Leyland Olympian on the 406 follows up behind. Both are crossing into Greater London near Tolworth. *John Glover*

might judge adequate for the public need, or otherwise. Inadequacy might be caused by a lack of an evening or weekend service, buses not serving all the points that previous practice had found necessary, or frequencies too low to cater adequately for traffic volumes or public need. Was there enough capacity to provide for the school elements? Were the smaller villages bypassed, or was there any bus service at all, anywhere near them?

If service registrations revealed that there would be 'on the road' competition between operators, this was one of the intentions of the 1985 Act and merely something to record. Competition was felt likely to be in the interests of the public in terms of the service quality and perhaps prices that they would be offered.

County Council actions

None of the above was a matter for the County Councils to make comment, save only for the inadequacies which they might find in the patterns of the services registered. This required (and still does require) an analysis of the shortcomings, and how additional services might best be provided to supplement the commercial network.

These thoughts then had to be turned into positive proposals to let contracts for services which were not provided. Specific requirements of the Act were that such contracts should be let on a competitive basis open to all who were technically qualified to be considered, and that the Councils, in devising the service details of what they required, must not do so in a way that inhibited competition.

In fact, the Act went rather further, and County Councils were obliged to make a formal statement of their public transport policies for buses (Appendix C). This was to enable bus operators to judge whether or not the services that they registered would be sufficient to deter the County Council from spending public money on service supplementation in some form. From their point of view, more buses chasing a similar number of passengers in total means less revenue per bus.

The successful bidder for the contract would then register the service in the same way as for a commercial one.

The letting of the contracts for what became known as the 'socially necessary services' determined what would be operated on the road on deregulation day, 26 October 1986, and for the three months that followed. From 26 January 1987, operators were able to introduce new services where they saw an opportunity, or were free to alter their existing services. However, for any alterations, they had to give the Traffic Commissioner 42 days' notice. The importance of the notice period was that it gave County Councils time to assess the effects of the alterations and to tender for an alternative facility if this was felt to be necessary.

There were additional complications if services crossed the boundary into Greater London; the out-county part would need to be registered but the London part also needed an agreement with what was by now London Regional Transport. This was the successor body to the London Transport Executive set up in 1984, and once again reporting to the Minister. Services within London were also being put out to tender, but in a regulated environment. There was no free competition. London Country and its successor companies were amongst those bidding to run routes within London, with some success.

SUPPORT SERVICES

Changes of this magnitude have other implications. Who, for instance, looks after the bus stops? Surrey took the view that operators would remain responsible for the erection and maintenance of poles, flags and timetables on all bus stops serving commercial services. Where a contract service was to use the same stop, the County Council would hope to negotiate with the existing operator for the display of service details and publicity material. The contract service(s) might, or might not, be run by the same operator. Where commercial services were withdrawn without replacement, the operator would be responsible for the removal of the stop.

At stops where there was no commercial service operating the County Council would seek to purchase and then maintain them. These stops would carry a 'Surrey County Council' sticker without a reference to the operator.

Of rather more significance was the provision of service publicity. Individual operators were clearly not going to provide it other than for their own services, and newcomers to bus operation in particular were unlikely to have much knowledge of what was involved. The immediate publicity requirement covered a telephone helpline for the public to find out what was happening to their bus services in the sense of timetable enquiries, the provision of printed information at bus stops, the availability of timetable books, and general publicity. This was to be made available as a printed A2 sheet in colour which was delivered to every household in the County, advertising on commercial radio stations and in the local press and at bus shelters, together with press releases.

Surrey decided initially that six timetable books to cover the County should be produced in which all services in the geographical areas concerned should be included — both commercial and socially necessary. The very tight timescales meant that production times and thus artwork had to be kept to a minimum, but later editions included town maps and other useful additions, as well as maps of the area covered overall.

It was felt that timetables should be distributed as widely as possible and the help of outlets from Council Offices and libraries to sub post offices was enlisted. The commercial strategy was to include a cover price on the timetable but make them available free to retail outlets; it was up to them whether to give them away or charge the cover price.

Success was demonstrated by the high take-up for the timetables, at a total of 200,000 for the six areas, with third editions of four of the six being required within a year. There was also heavy usage of the telephone hotline. The necessity for County Councils to involve themselves in the publicity efforts was amply demonstrated.

REGISTRATIONS

By February 1986, all bus operators were required to register those services that they were prepared to operate on a commercial basis from 26 October that year. As was anticipated, registrations in Surrey were confined to those who had previously been operating local bus services in the County, so there were no newcomers.

More surprising though was the level of commercial mileage it was intended to operate. The consultants Booz Allen & Hamilton, who had been retained by the Council in 1985 to prepare a report on the likely implications of deregulation, forecast that 45% of the mileage would be commercial. Instead, roughly 75% or 160,000 miles a week was registered, though direct comparisons were difficult. Where London Regional Transport services were concerned the distinction was not valid.

London Country South West became London & Country; this is one of its new Dennis Falcon single-deckers on the 414 to Croydon, photographed at Goodwyns in August 1990. Bodywork was by East Lancs, associated with LCSW's owner Drawlane, whose managing director was one Geoffrey Hilditch, well known for his penchant for Dennis products. Ray Stenning of Best Impressions had developed this new livery for the company. *Barry Le Jeune*

The pattern of commercial registrations, in many cases, differed radically from previous services. Some frequencies were increased or decreased, and many routes were altered to serve different areas, or truncated to leave other areas totally unserved. It followed that many poorly used services were not registered at all, especially evening and Sunday services.

The commercial registrations saw the emergence of a limited number of new minibus networks, which sought to increase patronage by providing high frequency, new routeings and better penetration of housing estates. The success of such schemes depended on substantial passenger generation and lower operating costs, but they still needed to be regarded as experimental. London Country South West registered 6,500 miles of weekly minibus operations.

An interesting feature of these new services was an attempt to carry out more sustained and effective marketing campaigns. However, the ability of minibuses to penetrate housing estates previously impassable to buses led to new problems as residents of many areas were now demanding bus services which previously would have been impractical. Conversely, other residents complained about intrusion.

Deregulation in Surrey did not lead to any new commercial operators offering services, though both Epsom Buses and East Surrey Buses started small-scale commercial local bus services as a supplement to their contracted operations.

A study of the financial performance of individual routes in Surrey prior to deregulation showed that several routes, registered as commercially viable by operators, were unlikely to prove so. Thus it had to be assumed that some of the commercial registrations were made in an attempt to pre-empt the emergence of competition. The 12 months following deregulation saw some of these routes withdrawn, suggesting a harder commercial attitude.

COMPETITION

There were relatively few cases of commercial competition in Surrey. The first example as a direct result of the 1985 Act arose between London Country South West operating the 406 between Epsom and Kingston, and London Buses, who attempted to compete over the same route but numbered 306. The LCSW

The former London Country companies tried minibuses as a competitive tool. Most were fairly mainstream, though Kentish Bus opted for these unusal three-axle Talbot minibuses, as seen on the 21 at Sevenoaks bus station. Kentish Bus's image was a long way removed from London Country, with its new name and maroon and cream livery. *Barry Le Jeune*

registration was for a service every 20min between Kingston and Tadworth with peak services continuing to Redhill, and a more restricted service in the evenings. Sunday services were hourly, to Tadworth only. In all cases, services operated for the full working day.

London Buses' registration was for a flat service from 07.30 to 18.30, running at 30min headways between Kingston and Epsom only on Mondays to Saturdays. No Sunday service was offered. It was deregistered three months later.

A significant development was what might be described as 'jockeying for position', that fell short of actual on-the-road competition. Thus both London Country South West and Epsom Buses proposed to introduce minibuses between the Merland Rise area of Tadworth and Epsom, but Epsom Buses withdrew its registration when it became aware of London Country's plans.

CONTRACTS

Socially necessary services were identified to the extent of 70,000 bus miles a week. Despite the multitude of additions and deletions of service which occurred in the first 12 months after deregulation, it was judged that the socially necessary services managed to preserve, and in some cases enhance, the total journey opportunities for the passenger.

There are essentially two sorts of contracts. These are:

- Minimum Cost, in which the operator is reimbursed with the full cost of operating the service and the County Council effectively retains the revenue. The Council therefore needs to specify the fares and conditions of travel, and takes the revenue risk. This is the type of contract which has been used generally in London
- Minimum Subsidy, in which the operator is reimbursed for the net cost after taking revenue into account. This can have various arrangements for fares:
     No fares specified by tendering authority
     Tendering authority specifies minimum and/or maximum fares
     Tendering authority specifies a fares scale.

Most of London Country South West's minibuses were Mercedes, though it did have eight Freight Rover Sherpa 16-seaters for its Horsham Minis service. S2 works an H3 town service in Horsham in March 1987. *Barry Le Jeune*

Surrey adopted the Minimum Subsidy type, with the Council specifying a maximum fare over a given range of distances. Minimum Cost contracts have their attractions, but they bring with them the necessity of the Council having to ensure that fares are collected, and that the revenue is actually received. This means regular revenue audit checks are required, with a consequent increase in either the duties and responsibilities of the Council's bus inspectorate, whose main concern is operational performance, or the employment of a separate group of people to check revenue collection. Either way, there was a manpower implication.

The contract period was set initially for a maximum of three years.

Competition for contracts was more marked than on-the-road commercial competition. Before contracts were awarded, the potential operator had to satisfy the Council that the company was in possession of an operator's licence, had the appropriate vehicles, had adequate maintenance facilities, and proper management control. Newcomers to local bus service operation were, if a contract was pending, visited to verify credentials and assessed as to their capability to fulfil the terms of the contract. The majority were already known to the Council as operators of school contracts, but public bus service operation has significant additional responsibilities. Broadly, the existing large companies lost some ground to the smaller companies in contract service provision.

Of the contract expenditure in Surrey during 1987/88 of £2,244,000, London Country South West accounted for £1,004,000, or 45% of the total.

RESOURCES

The resources requirements both in terms of vehicles and manpower was a variable dependent on the time of day and day of the week. The total vehicle requirement at the height of the morning peak, the most critical time, was estimated as follows:

Vehicles operating commercial local services in Surrey	325
Vehicles on local service contracts to Surrey County Council	80
Coaches operating school contracts for Surrey County Council	160
Minibuses operating school contracts for Surrey County Council	60
Total vehicle requirement	625

Other demands at such times are private schools and works contracts. Together, such commitments stretched operator resources to a point where response to tenders from the County Council for bus services and school contracts was often low and in some cases none at all. On average, 30 invitations to tender were sent out, with the number of replies roundly four. The emphasis was on the shortage of resources.

Contrary to expectations, the overall mileage in Surrey taking both commercial and contracted local services together, increased following deregulation: the January 1987 date marked the end of the freeze period during which no changes to registrations were allowed.

Surrey bus operations over the deregulation period, commercial and tendered services combined

Miles operated per week

	1 September 1986		26 January 1987		1 October 1987	
London Country	121,752	55%	112,091	47.8%	117,332	48.4%
Other operators	99,616	45%	122,410	52.2%	125,089	51.6%
Total mileage	221,368	100%	234,501	100%	242,421	100%
As index	100		105.9		109.5	

Thus in volume terms, London Country lost ground a little in the first phase, but much of this was regained at the end of the first year. However, this has to be set against an overall market growth of nearly 10% during the same period.

The reasons for the growth were ascribed to high-frequency minibuses displacing conventional buses at lower frequencies, and also the concentration of commercial operations in major corridors at certain times. This still required the County Council to supplement these services at other periods.

BUS COMPANY SALE

The Government was wary about the valuations to be attached to properties in areas such as the Home Counties when the companies were put up for sale. This especially affected bus garages and bus stations with high potential development value. It would not be in the public interest to dispose of potentially valuable sites at current use values, but nor was it practicable to expect buyers to purchase them at prices reflecting redevelopment values.

The four London Country operating companies occupied numerous sites of this nature around London and the M25. The properties were thus marketed separately from the companies. This arrangement did not prevent the bus operators and others from making inclusive bids for the companies and the properties, but it was designed to give committed bus operators a greater chance of bidding successfully for the bus business by guaranteeing them tenure of their depots for varying periods of up to 20 years, while at the same time realising the best overall proceeds for NBC on the sale. In the event, only London Country South West was sold separately from its properties.

Each LCBS operating company sale also included a share in Green Line Travel Ltd.

An area timetable booklet as produced by London Country for the Dorking and Reigate area, 1982. *John Glover*

THE OUTCOME

London Country Bus (North West) Ltd was sold to a management team of four on 5 January 1988. The sale included the freehold properties and a share in Green Line Travel Ltd. The headquarters was at Garston.

The company undertook the operation of bus and minibus services in West Hertfordshire, South Buckinghamshire, East Berkshire and North London, and was also a major contributor to the Green Line coach network. At the time of sale, LCNW had 360 vehicles and employed 1,040 staff.

London Country Bus (South West) Ltd was sold to Drawlane Ltd, a subsidiary of Endless Holdings, Salisbury, on 19 February 1988. Garage sites were sold separately to a subsidiary of Speyhawk Land & Estates Ltd, who signed lease agreements for continued operational use for designated periods. None of these, it turned out, exceeded 10 years. The headquarters remained that of LCBS, at Reigate. The company specialised in the operation of bus and minibus services in East Surrey and parts of West Sussex and South London. It also operated Flightlink and Speedlink airport services and was a major contributor to the Green Line coach network. At the time of sale, LCSW used 415 vehicles and employed 1,250 staff.

Gatwick Engineering Ltd was sold to Frontsource Group on 29 February 1988. This was the former Tinsley Lane company workshops outside Crawley, the completion of which in 1976 gave LCBS the capability to undertake major repairs and overhauls iself. The company undertook repairs, maintenance, overhaul, conversions, bodywork, unit reconditioning and spare parts supply for PSV and commercial vehicle businesses. At the time of sale, Tinsley Lane employed 150 staff.

Kentish Bus & Coach Co Ltd was sold to Proudmutual Ltd (the holding company for Northumbria Motor Services) on 15 March 1988. The sale included freehold properties and a share in Green Line Travel Ltd. The headquarters were at Northfleet.

This company was the operator of bus and coach services in West Kent and South East London, including services under contract to London Regional Transport. It was also a contributor to the Green Line coach network. At the time of sale, Kentish Bus & Coach used 168 vehicles and employed 512 staff.

London Country Bus (North East) Ltd was sold to Alan Stephenson and Parkdale Holdings PLC on 22 April 1988. The sale included freehold properties and a share in Green Line Travel Ltd. With headquarters at Hertford, LCNE operated buses and coaches in Central and East Hertfordshire, also Harlow and the Thurrock area of Essex. At the time of sale, 316 vehicles were used and 950 staff were employed.

The sale of Green Line Travel was completed on the same day, following the disposal of the last of the London Country operating subsidiaries.

In total the subsidiaries employed 3,902 staff and operated 1,259 vehicles.

London Country (North East) Ltd was the last of all the NBC operating companies to be sold. This left only Victoria Coach Station, which was disposed of to London Regional Transport on 31 October 1988.

NATIONAL AUDIT OFFICE

The National Audit Office later did a back check on the company sales, and one of those examined in detail was London Country North East. The following is taken from the NAO analysis:

This was termed 'a late sale of an unprofitable medium sized subsidiary'. Because there were a number of properties which would be worth more under alternative uses than as mere bus garages, it was decided to accept bids in three forms:

- For the property alone, subject to leases in favour of the operating subsidiary;
- For the bus operations alone; and
- For the property and bus operations combined.

Nine bids were received, but none was for the bus operational alone — even though the company had invited negative bids; NBC was prepared to pay somebody to acquire the business. As the disposal of the property on its own would have resulted in the break-up of the subsidiary, reducing both proceeds and competition, it was decided that the five combined bids only should be considered.

The sale included the freehold garages at Grays, Harlow, Hatfield, St Albans and Stevenage, and four leased properties. The alternative use value was thought to exceed the current use value (as garages) by £2.1m. The final offer comprised a premium bid for the freehold properties above their alternative use value, and a negative bid for the bus operation. The company considered that this final offer represented an overall premium of 6% over the net book value of the assets, and was a good price in the light of past results and projected losses. Taxation, employee participation and competition matters were also considered and found satisfactory.

The successful bidder found, upon detailed investigation, that a number of the properties marketed as freehold had defective titles. Furthermore, the subsidiary was continuing to make significant losses, although the company had indicated that these were under control and that bids should be made on that understanding. As a result, the company was forced to reopen negotiations with the successful bidder, accept a reduction in the value offered for the property and agree to bear the losses between the original strike date in June 1987 and the revised date in February 1988. The subsidiary was subsequently sold for a sum which represented some 40% of the original offer (although still a 6% premium over net book value).

The alternatives of remarketing the company, delaying its sale and breaking it up were rejected as unlikely to produce a better result. The net proceeds of the sale of London Country North East were £3.6 million, against the net book value of the assets of £3.4 million. The break-up value was put at £3 million.

COMMERCIAL SERVICE OUTLOOK

The future of the commercially registered network, as seen in Surrey from a year after deregulation, appeared to depend on a number of factors.

What would be the profitability, or not as the case might be, of the service provision? It was thought that the required rate of return on capital invested might well alter as a result in the change of ownership of the London Country derivatives and the other former NBC companies.

Would the bus companies be able to retain the then current revenue levels or, at least, meet minimum revenue projections? Some evidence of fares rises in excess of the rate of inflation indicated potential problems in this area.

Could the bus companies make savings on their variable and semi-variable costs? This was particularly important for the larger companies, where this would typically take place through productivity wage agreements and a more flexible use of staff and vehicle resources.

Could they also make savings in their fixed costs, again mainly a problem for the larger companies? The Council recorded that the hiving off of the property assets of London Country South West 'would seem to preclude the company from benefiting in this respect'. This turned out to be a master of understatement in terms of what actually happened later.

Overall, it was then concluded that, while some stability might eventually emerge, this seemed likely to be at a rather lower level of service provision than was experienced initially.

CONTRACT SERVICES

Surrey's experience in the first year showed that the network of socially necessary services built up as a result of deregulation was soundly based. Only two operators felt obliged to terminate their contracts due to insufficient revenue, and in both cases there were significant other factors involved. The retendering process demonstrated that the great majority of original prices were realistic. While some retendered costs were greater than purely the effects of inflation, this was more than balanced by savings through the specification of minibuses for the less well used contracted services.

The response to tendering of local bus services was in many cases significantly better than the response to tenders for school bus services. This might have been because the construction of local bus service tenders aimed to maximise vehicle utilisation, which was in the interests of both the County Council and the operators. The emergence of coach operators new to the provision of local bus services was to be welcomed and encouraged. The existence of a number of companies able to take on additional commitments was felt to be of great benefit should any of the larger companies reduce their fleet sizes through circumstances beyond their control.

The 727 Green Line resorted to Leyland Nationals on this occasion with London Country North East SNB303 climbing out of Surbiton on a southbound journey to Crawley in June 1987 in the rather attractive livery adopted by the North East company after privatisation. *John Glover*

It was in tendering authorities' interests to foster good relations with all companies through the tendering system and the operation of the various concessionary schemes. The privatisation of the NBC companies was felt likely to lead to the breakdown of long-established territorial boundaries between the companies and a consequent increase in competition to secure County Council contracts.

Since deregulation, the County Councils had largely been compelled to adopt a reactive posture over the provision of local bus services; that is, to fill the socially necessary gaps that the commercial market would not provide. While such a reactive role was unavoidable in that changes in commercial services would have to be considered and perhaps met by amendment to or expansion of contract services, this was essentially a negative approach. There was much to be said for taking a more proactive role and trying to influence events.

THE FUTURE, SEEN FROM 1987

Bus service provision was continuing to change, and there were many potential problems to be faced in the future:

- The demand for buses depends on demography, car ownership, land use, employment levels and location, retailing practice, disposable income and fuel prices. Few of these trends were helpful to the bus industry
- Most agreed that bus companies operating commercially would need to concentrate on major routes, leaving the marginal operation either to wither or be picked up by the tendering authorities. The ability of County Councils to let contracts was dependent upon budgetary considerations; at any one time there would be long-term contracts, with two or more years to run, those coming up for renewal, and new demands. Resolution of competing claims against a fixed financial ceiling would become increasingly difficult, and must involve a stricter interpretation of County Council policies for provision
- The instability brought about by (then) a 42-day forward commitment to providing bus services before competitive changes could be introduced, and the restructuring of the bus industry itself, would continue to be felt. Some companies would collapse. If larger companies went out of business, there would be little to replace them
- The relationship between commercial and contracted services would undergo further change. Assuming that the operating companies would no longer be able or willing to indulge in a social conscience, this relationship would become more clear cut and was likely to give rise to yet more deregistrations of commercial services
- Parental choice of school was likely to result in a more dispersed pattern of journeys, over longer distances. This would bring new and greater demands on peak bus service provision.

9   **Conclusion**

'One of the greatest achievements of the National Bus Company was the conversion of London Country Buses, inherited in 1970 with an aged fleet and no cash, into an efficient and profitable enterprise, with the survival and major expansion of Green Line coach services.'

G. M. Newberry, NBC Director of Operational Development, 1974-79

By the early 1950s, the bus industry had largely recovered from the depredations of World War 2, and in many ways the outlook was rosy. But 1955 was to see the high point in terms of passenger carrying by the Country Bus & Coach department of the nationalised London Transport Executive. Thereafter followed a continuing downward trend in passenger volumes:

Passenger journeys by London Country Bus Services, and predecessor, selected years 1955 to 1985

1955	332 million
1969	198 million
1974	154 million
1985	106 million

By any standards, that was a huge reduction, with 40% of the loss occurring under London Transport ownership, and another third of the 1955 carryings while in the stewardship of the National Bus Company. Less than a third remained in the run-up to dismemberment of the company and the subsequent privatisation of its component parts.

That was accompanied by an equally daunting financial situation, partly perhaps self-inflicted by an inadequate appreciation of the predicament in which it found itself, but also what seemed to amount to a fudge in the transfer of what was to become London Country Bus Services Ltd to NBC in 1970. The emphasis of the legislation was clearly on getting London right. London Transport's Country Bus & Coach Department was a proportionately small part of the total business, and transfer to NBC solved the problem of political control for operations mainly outside Greater London and was administratively tidy.

But London Country was not a complete operation, with many shortcomings of which little attempt was made to put right as part of the transfer. Not the least of these was an ancient fleet in a company without proper workshops, and most of which dictated crew operation.

In the NBC parent company, the financial performance of LCBS with rates of pay and operating practices influenced by its previous history as part of London Transport was a cause of concern from the beginning. Thus the new Managing Director, Derek Fytche in 1976 was exhorted to 'do something, or consider closing it'. Underinvestment, obsolete operational methods, restrictive union agreements were all part of the problem. A new service network was needed, the routes must reach an adequate level of reliability, and employment conditions needing sorting out. That referred mainly to Green Line coach operations, but the bus side was equally challenging.

Where was the place of local authorities in this brave new world? Would the likes of Superbus in Stevenage be seen again? This is the SB2 route with London Country's very first Leyland National, LN1, at Stevenage bus station. Superbus evaluated both the Leyland National and its Anglo-Swedish rival, the Metro-Scania. *NBC/Ian Allan Library*

The decline in the rural bus in the 1950s resulted in the Jack Report in 1961, though it was another decade before Government found legislative time to produce an answer to what was seen as a problem limited to the countryside. This was the cue for the entry of the County Councils into the equation as a source of limited funding top-ups, but it was a task on which to cut their teeth. Local government reorganisation which took effect from 1974 was to give them much greater powers.

Òr was it? The duty of co-ordination of transport without any means of control does have its limitations. Again, it is perhaps fair to say that few had any real inkling as to how deep the industry problems lay, and nowhere more so than with London Country.

Seen from a County Council viewpoint, in this case Surrey County Council, there were five distinct phases in terms of the relationship with London Country, as follows:

1 First, in pre-1974 days, the County Council came to grips with its new but limited role in assessing the need for, and also paying, Rural Bus Grant for a small number of services. It also enabled it to work out what its objectives in spending public moneys were, and finding out what it was getting for its money by a survey programme

2 The second phase from 1974 to around 1978 saw the new Council's responsibilities and powers considerably enhanced. However, the ability to make substantial progress was largely thwarted by the need for both the Council and the company to come to grips with the inherited problems of LCBS, plus those brought about by falling traffic and rampant inflation. The underlying aim was to achieve some stability, on all counts

3 The third phase was that of steady and consistent progress, which sadly lasted only a few years until 1984 or so. This saw real development in policies which, it was hoped, might map a long-term future of the bus in Surrey

4 This gave way to the fourth phase, 1984-86, that of preparing for and coping with the deregulation of bus services and its execution, the letting of contracts and the splitting of the company

5 The fifth phase, from 1987, saw further adjustments in the light of experience, and the sale of the London Country subsidiaries to the private sector.

What then was the job of County Councils in the London Country years? As a former co-ordinator put it recently, 'managing decline, not always very successfully'.

That is one view, but is it really fair? The missing ingredient in this conclusion has been the staff of London Country Bus Services themselves. They were the ones who had the task of managing the company, not the County Councils. The latter were a new element in bus company life, starting with the rural bus grants on what were, admittedly, very minor services, which grew to an extent that the County Councils together controlled around a fifth of the company's total income through the grants that they could make available.

That London Country Bus Services, as a company, survived as well as it did and for as long as it did, was due principally to the efforts of its management and the staff. In negotiations and in planning meetings with County Councils, either side could, and did, bring bad news as well as good news, but there was always a willingness to pursue a joint approach to problems which concerned both parties. The relationship was always highly professional, and in those terms they were very good years indeed.

A diagram of the organisation of the Operating Department as it was in 1982 will be found in Appendix D.

Bus stations are useful infrastructure, but they add costs and may occupy commercially valuable space. This is the one in Redhill, with a 410 for Reigate approaching in January 1988. *John Glover*

Appendix A

The Routes

'The routes of the green Country Buses of London Transport cover 1,500 miles of road in London's country, its satellite towns, and its rural villages. They are integrated with the red Central Buses which cover all main roads in central and suburban London and with the Green Line Coaches which provide a luxury express service through and across the whole London Transport area.'

Thus, the July 1969 map for Country Buses issued by London Transport, and the last to be produced by that organisation. Subsequent changes before London Country assumed responsibility were few, but include the inauguration of Superbus services in Stevenage.

COUNTRY BUS ROUTES 1969

This list is shown in route numerical order and lists those operated. It does not give any indication of frequency of operation, nor the extent to which some buses may have been regularly terminated short. Thus of the six off-peak buses an hour leaving Kingston on the 406 service to Redhill in 1969, four terminated at Tadworth and only two continued to Redhill.

Omitted from this list are special routes serving mainly schools, hospitals and factories.

300	STIFFORD CLAYS, Socketts Heath, Grays, West Thurrock, PURFLEET
301	WATFORD HEATH or LITTLE BUSHEY, Watford, Kings Langley, Boxmoor, Berkhamsted, Tring, AYLESBURY
302	BENNETTS END, Adeyfield, Hemel Hempstead, Apsley, Kings Langley, Watford, WATFORD HEATH or LITTLE BUSHEY
303	NEW BARNET, Potters Bar, Bell Bar, Hatfield, Welwyn Garden City, Welwyn, Knebworth, Stevenage, HITCHIN
303A	NEW BARNET, Potters Bar, Brookmans Park Station, Hatfield, Welwyn Garden City, Welwyn, Knebworth, Stevenage, HITCHIN
304	COLNEY STREET, St Albans, Wheathampstead, Kimpton, Whitwell, HITCHIN
305	UXBRIDGE, Gerrards Cross, Chalfont St Peter, Chalfont St Giles, Seer Green, Beaconsfield, Loudwater, HIGH WYCOMBE
305A	UXBRIDGE, Gerrards Cross, Chalfont St Peter, CHALFONT COMMON
306	NEW BARNET, Barnet, Borehamwood, Elstree, Bushey Heath, Bushey, Watford, LEAVESDEN
307	HEMEL HEMPSTEAD STATION, Hemel Hempstead, Adeyfield, Redbourn, HARPENDEN (Masefield Road)
308	HERTFORD, Horns Mill, Bayford, Cuffley Station, GOFFS OAK
309	HAREFIELD (Hare End or St Mary's Road), Shrubs Corner, Rickmansworth, Mill End, CHORLEYWOOD (Furze View or The Gate)
309A	NORTHWOOD, Rickmansworth, then as 309 to CHORLEYWOOD (Furze View)

310	HERTFORD (Sele Farm Estate), Ware, Hoddesdon, Broxbourne, Waltham Cross, ENFIELD
310A	RYE HOUSE, Hoddesdon, thence as 310 to ENFIELD
311	SHENLEY, Radlett, Aldenham, Watford, LEAVESDEN
312	HEMEL HEMPSTEAD (Highfield), Two Waters, Boxmoor, Berkhamsted, DURRANTS FARM ESTATE
313	ENFIELD, Potters Bar, South Mimms, London Colney, ST ALBANS. Extended to WHIPSNADE PARK ZOO in the summer, stopping only at Redbourn and Markyate
314	HEMEL HEMPSTEAD STATION, Chaulden, Hemel Hempstead, Two Waters, APSLEY MILLS
314A	WARNERS END, Gadebridge, Hemel Hempstead, Moor End, BENNETTS GATE
315	HATFIELD, Welwyn Garden City, Hatfield, KIMPTON
315A	HATFIELD STATION, Welwyn Garden City, Welwyn, Woolmer Green, KNEBWORTH
317	HEMEL HEMPSTEAD STATION, Hemel Hempstead, Piccotts End, Water End, Great Gaddesden, Ringshall, Northchurch, BERKHAMSTED
317A	TWO WATERS, Boxmoor, Hemel Hempstead, Piccotts End, Water End, Nettleden, Little Gaddesden, Ringshall, Northchurch, BERKHAMSTED
318	ABBOTS LANGLEY, Garston, Watford, Croxley Green, Sarratt, Chipperfield, Bovingdon, Boxmoor, HEMEL HEMPSTEAD
318A	ABBOTS LANGLEY, Garston, Watford, Croxley Green, BUCKS HILL
319	CHIPPERFIELD, Kings Langley, Abbots Langley, Garston, WATFORD
320	GADEBRIDGE, Boxmoor, Hemel Hempstead, Adeyfield, LEVERSTOCK GREEN (Woolmer Drive)

Green Line RMC1519 at Golders Green in the latter days of London Transport ownership sees service on Route 716. It is about to depart for Chertsey on 9 April 1969 with a load which would be unheard of in the not-too-distant future. *John Glover*

321	LUTON, Kinsbourne Green, Harpenden, St Albans, St Stephens, Garston, Watford, Croxley, Rickmansworth, Maple Cross, Denham, UXBRIDGE. Additional service: LUTON-RICKMANSWORTH (Berry Lane Estate)
322	WATFORD JUNCTION, Huntonbridge, Kings Langley Station, Hemel Hempstead, HIGHFIELD
322A	WATFORD JUNCTION, Huntonbridge, Kings Langley Station, Hemel Hempstead, WARNER'S END
323	GRAYS, Woodside Estate, CHADWELL ST MARY (Alexandra Close)
324	WELWYN GARDEN CITY TOWN SERVICE
325	NEW GREENS ESTATE, St Albans, COTTONMILL ESTATE
326	MILL END ROAD, High Wycombe, MICKLEFIELD ESTATE
327	HERTFORD, Ware, St Margarets, Hoddesdon, Broxbourne, Nazeingbury, Nazeingwood Common, NAZEING
328	RAINHAM or AVELEY (Usk Road), Belhus, North Stifford, Grays, STIFFORD CLAYS
328A	STIFFORD CLAYS, Socketts Heath, Grays, Belhus, Aveley, PURFLEET
329	HERTFORD, Bramfield, Datchfield, Knebworth, NUP END
330	HOWLANDS or GREAT GANETT, Welwyn Garden City, Hatfield, Smallford, St Albans, Leverstock Green, HEMEL HEMPSTEAD
330A	HOWLANDS, Welwyn Garden City, Lemsford Lane, Hatfield, St Albans, Leverstock Green, HEMEL HEMPSTEAD

331	HERTFORD, Ware, Wadesmill, Standon, Puckeridge, West Mill, BUNTINGFORD
331A	HERTFORD, Ware, Wadesmill, Standon, Puckeridge, Hare Street, BUNTINGFORD
333	HERTFORD, Bengeo, CHAPMORE END or MOLE WOOD ESTATE
333B	HERTFORD, Bengeo, WARE PARK HOSPITAL
335	WATFORD, Croxley, Rickmansworth, Chorleywood, Chenies, Chalfont St Giles, Gerrards Cross, Fulmer, Slough, WINDSOR
336	WATFORD, Watford Met Station, Croxley, Rickmansworth, Chorleywood Station, Chenies, Amersham (Oakfield Corner), CHESHAM
336A	RICKMANSWORTH, LOUDWATER ESTATE
337	DUNSTABLE, Whipsnade Heath, Studham, Water End, Hemel Hempstead, HEMEL HEMPSTEAD STATION
338	RADLETT, Harperbury Hospital, London Colney, ST ALBANS
338A	RADLETT, Harperbury Hosp, Napsbury Hospital, ST ALBANS
339	WARLEY, Brentwood, Chipping Ongar, North Weald, Epping, Potter Street, Old Harlow, HARLOW BUS STATION
340A	SOUTH HATFIELD, Hatfield, Howlands, Welwyn Garden City, HALDENS or PANSHANGER
340B	NEW BARNET, North Mymms, South Hatfield, HATFIELD (Birchwood Estate)
341	ST ALBANS (Marshalwick Estate), Fleetville, Smallford, Hatfield, Essendon Mill, Horns Mill, HERTFORD
341B	ST ALBANS (Marshalwick Estate), Fleetville, Smallford, Hatfield, Woods Avenue, SOUTH HATFIELD

The RP Park Royal-bodied AEC Reliances had a short stay on Green Line; here one in NBC 'local coach' livery departs from Cobham on the 715 for Hertford. *Ian Allan Library*

371	TILBURY, Grays, West Thurrock, Stonehouse Corner, Aveley, Tunnel Garage, Wennington, RAINHAM
371A	TILBURY, Grays, West Thurrock, Stonehouse Corner, PURFLEET
371B	TILBURY, Grays, West Thurrock, Stonehouse Corner, Aveley, Sandy Lane, Wennington, RAINHAM
373	PENN and BEACONSFIELD
374	LINFORD, East Tilbury, Chadwell St Mary, Grays, West Thurrock, Stonehouse Corner, Uplands Estate, RAINHAM
380	HARLOW (Bus Station), Mark Hall South, HARLOW (Mark Hall North)
381	EASTWICK, Harlow, Tylerscross, Epping, TOOT HILL or COOPERSALE COMMON (Circular)
382	ST ALBANS, Astwick Manor, Lemsford, Welwyn, CODICOTE
383	OAKFIELD ESTATE, Hitchin, Willian, WESTON. Additional Service: OAKFIELD ESTATE (Hitchin)-PURWELL LANE ESTATE
384	LETCHWORTH, Willian, Graveley, Stevenage, Walkern, Benington, Dane End, Tonwell, Ware, HERTFORD
384A	GREAT MUNDEN, Dane End, Tonwell, Ware, HERTFORD
385	WATFORD BYPASS (Savage & Parson's), Millway Estate, Watford, HOLYWELL ESTATE, or Croxley Green, Rickmansworth, BERRY LANE ESTATE
385A	GARSTON, Meriden Estate, Watford, then as Route 385
386	BISHOP'S STORTFORD (Havers Lane Estate), Little Hadham, Standon, Braughing, Hare Street, Buntingford, Cromer, Walkern, Stevenage, Great Wymondley, HITCHIN on Saturdays. Runs from Hertford via Ware to Standon, thence as above to Hitchin on Tuesdays and to Bishop's Stortford on Thursdays
387	TRING, Tring Station, ALDBURY
388	HARLOW, Stanstead Abbots, St Margarets, Ware, Hertford, Tewin, Welwyn North Station, MARDLEY HILL or WELWYN GARDEN CITY
389	WARE STATION and KINGSHILL ESTATE (Circular)
390	SAWBRIDGEWORTH, High Wych, Eastwick, Harlow Bus Station, Tylerscross, Roydon, St Margarets, Ware, Hertford, Stapleford, Watton, Bragbury End, Aston, Broadwater, STEVENAGE
391	TYTTENHANGER or MILE HOUSE ESTATE, Hill End, St Albans, FIRBANK ROAD
391A	HILL END, St Albans, NEW GREENS ESTATE
393	WELWYN GARDEN CITY (Lemsford Lane), Hertingfordbury, Hertford, Hertford Heath, Hoddesdon, Broxbourne, Clay Hill, Tylerscross, HARLOW BUS STATION
393A	WELWYN GARDEN CITY STATION, Hertingfordbury, Hertford, Hertford Heath, Hoddesdon, Broxbourne, Nazeingwood Common, Tylerscross, HARLOW BUS STATION
394	TRING, Wiggington, Cholesbury, Chesham, Chartridge, Lee Common, GREAT MISSENDEN. Certain buses run by way of Swan Bottom Cross Roads and The Lee
395	WARE (Fanshawe Crescent), Ware, HERTFORD (Sele Farm Estate)
395A	FANHAM COMMON, Ware, HERTFORD (Sele Farm Estate)
396	EPPING STATION, Potter Street, Old Harlow, Sawbridgeworth, BISHOP'S STORTFORD
397	STEWARDS (Circular), Passmores, Harlow Bus Station, Old Harlow, BISHOP'S STORTFORD. Additional service: PASSMORES-OLD HARLOW (Mulberry Green) (via First Avenue)
397A	STEWARDS (Circular), Passmores, Harlow Bus Station, Old Harlow, BISHOP'S STORTFORD (via Temple Fields)
398	AMERSHAM (Quill Hall Estate), Coleshill, BEACONSFIELD
400	BRITWELL, Salt Hill, Slough, Upton Lea, Wexham Court Farm Estate, Slough, Salt Hill, BRITWELL
401	UPPER or LOWER BELVEDERE, Bexleyheath, Bexley, Dartford Heath, Dartford, Wilmington, Sutton-at-Hone, Farningham, Shoreham, Otford, SEVENOAKS
401A	BEXLEYHEATH, Bexley, or DARTFORD to JOYDENS WOOD ESTATE
402	BROMLEY, Bromley Common, Farnborough, Green St Green, Knockholt Station, Polhill, Dunton Green, Riverhead, Sevenoaks, Hildenborough, TONBRIDGE
403	WALLINGTON, Beddington, Croydon, Sanderstead, Warlingham, Chelsham, Westerham, Brasted, Riverhead, Sevenoaks, Hildenborough, TONBRIDGE
403A	WALLINGTON, Beddington, Croydon, Sanderstead, Warlingham, Chelsham, WARLINGHAM PARK HOSPITAL
403B	WALLINGTON, Beddington, Croydon, Sanderstead, Warlingham, Chelsham, FARLEIGH
404	SHOREHAM VILLAGE, Otford, SEVENOAKS
405	WEST CROYDON, Purley, Coulsdon, Merstham, Redhill, Earlswood, Horley, Gatwick Airport, CRAWLEY
405B	REDHILL, Earlswood, Horley, Gatwick Airport, Manor Royal, Crawley, then circular via Furnace Green and Tilgate
406	KINGSTON, Surbiton, Tolworth, Ewell, Epsom, Tattenham Corner, Tadworth, Kingswood, Reigate, REDHILL
406A	KINGSTON, Surbiton, Tolworth, Ewell, Epsom, Tattenham Corner, Merland Rise, Tadworth, Kingswood, Reigate, REDHILL
406F	EPSOM and EPSOM DOWNS
407	LANGLEY VILLAGE, Slough, CIPPENHAM
408	FARLEIGH or WARLINGHAM PARK HOSPITAL, Chelsham, Warlingham, Sanderstead, Croydon, Beddington, Wallington, Sutton, Cheam, Ewell, Epsom, Leatherhead, Bookham, East Horsley, Merrow, GUILDFORD
408A	GUILDFORD and MERROW (Bushey Hill)
409	West Croydon, Purley, Old Coulsdon, Caterham, Godstone, Blindley Heath, Lingfield, Felbridge, East Grinstead, FOREST ROW
410	BROMLEY, Bromley Common, Keston, Biggin Hill, Westerham, Limpsfield, Oxted, Godstone, Nutfield, Redhill, REIGATE
411	WEST CROYDON, Purley, Old Coulsdon, Caterham, Godstone, Nutfield, Redhill, REIGATE
412	RANMORE, Dorking, Westcott, Wotton Hatch, Abinger, Holmbury St Mary, SUTTON
413	CHIPSTEAD (or SHOREHAM, Otford), Riverhead, Sevenoaks, Cross Keys, Ide Hill, BRASTED
414	WEST CROYDON, Purley, Coulsdon, Merstham, Redhill, Reigate, Betchworth, Dorking, Beare Green, Capel, Warnham, HORSHAM
415	GUILDFORD, Burpham/Burnt Common, RIPLEY

Right: Former Green Line RCL2259, now with London Country fleetnames, was on relatively mundane duties on the 405 when pictured in Redhill High Street on 25 October 1977. *Guy Brigden*

Below: The diversion round Berrylands on the 418 is seen here on 20 August 1977 with SM107 on its way to Kingston. *Guy Brigden*

416	TADWORTH, Walton-on-the-Hill, Headley, Leatherhead, Oxshott, ESHER. Certain buses run from Pebblecombe to Boxhill (Greenacres)
417	LANGLEY VILLAGE, Slough, Windsor, OLD WINDSOR HOSPITAL
418	KINGSTON, Surbiton, Berrylands, Tolworth, West Ewell, Epsom, Leatherhead, Great Bookham, BOOKHAM STATION
419	LANGLEY VALE, Epsom, Long Grove Hospital, BRETTGRAVE
420	WOKING, Sheerwater Estate, WEST BYFLEET
421	HEVERHAM, Kemsing, Otford, SEVENOAKS
422	LEATHERHEAD, Headley, Pebblecombe, BOXHILL (Greenacres)
423	WROTHAM, West Kingsdown, Farningham, Swanley, Birchwood, Dartford Heath, Wilmington, Dartford, Southern Hospital, Watchgate, Green St Green, LONGFIELD
424	REIGATE, Woodhatch, Sidlow, Duxhurst or Irons Bottom, Hookwood, Horley, Smallfield, Copthorne, Snow Hill or Crawley Down, Felbridge, EAST GRINSTEAD (Stone Quarry Estate)
425	DORKING, Westcott, Abinger Hammer, Shere, Albury, Shalford, GUILDFORD
426	CRAWLEY, Three Bridges, Tinsley Green, Horley, Povey Cross, Charlwood, Ifield Wood, Ifield, CRAWLEY (Circular)

426A	POUND HILL, Three Bridges, Crawley, IFIELD
427	WOKING, Maybury Inn, Pyrford, West Byfleet, Byfleet, New Haw, ADDLESTONE
428	DORMANSLAND, Lingfield, Felcourt, EAST GRINSTEAD
430	REDHILL, Earlswood, Woodhatch, South Park, REIGATE
431	ORPINGTON, Chelsfield, Halstead, Knockholt Pound, Dunton Green, Riverhead, SEVENOAKS
432	GREAT BOOKHAM, Little Bookham, Effingham, Horsley, Merrow, GUILDFORD
434	HORSHAM, Littlehaven, Faygate, Crawley, Three Bridges, Copthorne, Crawley Down, Turner's Hill, East Grinstead, Dormansland, EDENBRIDGE
435	EAST GRINSTEAD and IMBERHORNE ESTATE
436	STAINES, Chertsey, Addlestone, New Haw, Woodham, Woking, Send, Burnt Common, Burpham, GUILDFORD
436A	STAINES, Chertsey, Addlestone, New Haw, Woodham, Woking, Send, Send Marsh, RIPLEY
437	WOKING, Maybury Inn, West Byfleet, Byfleet, New Haw, ADDLESTONE
438A	CRAWLEY, Three Bridges, Copthorne, Crawley Down, Felbridge, EAST GRINSTEAD
439	REDHILL, Wray Common, Reigate, Leigh, Gadbrook, thence circular via Brockham Green, Dorking, Holmwood, Beare Green, Newdigate, Brockham Green, DORKING
440	WOLDINGHAM, Caterham, Chaldon Cross Roads, Merstham, South Merstham, Redhill, Earlswood, SALFORDS
441	STAINES, Pooley Green, Egham, Old Windsor, Windsor, Slough, Hedgerley Corner, Beaconsfield, Wycombe Marsh, HIGH WYCOMBE Additional service: as above to Hedgerley Corner, thence to HEDGERLEY VILLAGE
441A	STAINES, Pooley Green, Egham, ENGLEFIELD GREEN (Cherrywood Avenue)
442	HIGH WYCOMBE and HICKS FARM ESTATE (Circular)
444	STAINES, Stanwell Moor, STAINES
445	DATCHET, Eton, WINDSOR
446	SLOUGH, Whitby Road, FARNHAM ROAD

Left: RMC1509 looks sprucely turned out for the 315A to Woolmer Green. *Author's collection*

Right: This RF, on a 708 to Hemel Hempstead, has lost all obvious affiliations with London Transport, but it couldn't have come from anywhere else! *Author's collection*

Below right: GS42, with GS33 forming a relief, are seen at Rickmansworth station on the 336A to Loudwater Village. *Ian Allan Library*

446a	SLOUGH, Manor Park, FARNHAM ROAD
447	REDHILL, Batts Hill, Reigate, Meadvale, Earlswood, Redhill, South Merstham, MERSTHAM (Delabole Road)
449	SOUTH HOLMWOOD, Dorking, (Goodwyns Farm Estate), Chart Downs Estate, HOLMWOOD COMMON (Four Wents Pond)
450	DARTFORD, Greenhithe, Bean, Betsham, GRAVESEND
451	HARTLEY COURT, Hartley, Longfield, Westwood, Betsham, GRAVESEND
452	DARTFORD, Greenhithe, Bean, Westwood, Longfield, Fawkham Green, WEST KINGSDOWN
453	CHELSHAM, Warlingham, Whyteleafe, CATERHAM
454	CHIPSTEAD, Riverhead, Sevenoaks, Weald, Hildenborough, TONBRIDGE
455	UXBRIDGE, Gerrards Cross, Beaconsfield, Wycombe Marsh, HIGH WYCOMBE
456	WOKING, Maybury Inn, Pyrford, West Byfleet, Woodham, New Haw, ADDLESTONE
457	UXBRIDGE, Iver Heath, Slough, WINDSOR
457A	UXBRIDGE, Iver Heath, Upton Lea, Slough, WINDSOR
458	UXBRIDGE, Iver, Langley, SLOUGH
459	UXBRIDGE, Iver, RICHINGS PARK
460	STAINES, Wraysbury, Datchet Common, Datchet, SLOUGH
461	STAINES, Chertsey, Addlestone, Weybridge, WALTON-ON-THAMES
461A	BOTLEY'S PARK (St Peter's Hospital), Ottershaw, Addlestone, Weybridge, WALTON-ON-THAMES
462	LEATHERHEAD, Fetcham, Cobham, Weybridge, ADDLESTONE
463	WALTON-ON-THAMES, Weybridge, Addlestone, New Haw, Woodham, Woking, Send, Burnt Common, West Clandon, Merrow, GUILDFORD
464	HOLLAND, Hurst Green, Oxted, Limpsfield, Kent Hatch, Crockham Hill, WESTERHAM. Additional service: OXTED-GORDONS WAY
465	HOLLAND, Hurst Green, Oxted, Limpsfield, Kent Hatch, Crockham Hill, EDENBRIDGE
466	STAINES, Egham, Stroude, KNOWLE HILL
467	SIDCUP, Foots Cray, Bexley, Crayford, Dartford, Wilmington, Sutton-at-Hone, South Darenth, HORTON KIRBY
468	EPSOM, Ewell, West Ewell, CHESSINGTON ZOO
469	STAINES, Pooley Green, Thorpe, VIRGINIA WATER
470	WARLINGHAM PARK HOSPITAL or FARLEIGH, Chelsham, Warlingham, Sanderstead, Croydon, Beddington, Wallington, Sutton, Cheam, Ewell, Epsom, Leatherhead, Boxhill, DORKING
471	ORPINGTON, Green Street Green, Cudham, Knockholt, Pratt's Bottom, Green Street Green, ORPINGTON (Circular)
472	LEATHERHEAD, Epsom, Ewell, Cheam, Sutton, Wallington, NETHERNE HOSPITAL (Limited Stop Service)
473	HORSHAM, Littlehaven, Faygate, Crawley, Three Bridges, Turner's Hill, East Grinstead, DORMANSLAND
476	IFIELD (The Parade), Langley Green, Crawley, Southgate Avenue, thence circular via Furnace Green and Tilgate
477	DARTFORD, Wilmington, Hextable, Swanley, Crockenhill, St Mary Cray, Orpington, CHELSFIELD
480	DENTON, Gravesend, Northfleet, Swanscombe, Greenhithe, Dartford, Crayford, Slade Green, ERITH
481	EPSOM and WELLS ESTATE
482	CATERHAM STATION, Godstone, Bletchingley, Nutfield, Redhill, Horley, SMALLFIELD HOSPITAL
484	LANGLEY VILLAGE, Parlaunt Estate, Slough, Salt Hill, FARNHAM ROAD
484A	DATCHET, Langley, Slough, Salt Hill, FARNHAM ROAD
485	WESTERHAM, Crockham Hill, EDENBRIDGE
486	DARTFORD (Bow Arrow Lane), Dartford, Crayford, Bexleyheath, UPPER BELVEDERE
487	SWANSCOMBE, Northfleet, Gravesend, Gypsy Corner, SINGLEWELL or KINGS FARM ESTATE
489	ASH, Hartley, Longfield, Westwood, Southfleet, GRAVESEND

489A	MEOPHAM (Hook Green), Longfield Hill, Longfield, Westwood, Southfleet, GRAVESEND	494	OXTED, Tandridge, Lingfield, Felcourt, EAST GRINSTEAD
490	GRAVESEND, Southfleet, New Barn, Longfield, Hartley, HARTLEY COURT	495	NORTHFLEET, Waterdales, Gravesend, KINGS FARM ESTATE
		496	NORTHFLEET, Gravesend, KINGS FARM ESTATE
491	LOWER BELVEDERE, Barnehurst, Perry Street, Crayford, Dartford, Wilmington, Sutton-at-Hone, HORTON KIRBY	498	GRAVESEND and PAINTERS ASH ESTATE or NORTHFLEET. Additional Service: GRAVESEND-COLDHARBOUR ESTATE
493	ORPINGTON (Ramsden Estate), Orpington Station, Chelsfield Station, GREEN STREET GREEN	499	JOYCE GREEN HOSPITAL, Temple Hill Estate, Dartford, Fleet Estate, DOWNS ESTATE

Left: This Crawley-based 479A is a SMW2, an ex-South Wales Willowbrook-bodied Swift, bound for Gossops Green.
Author's collection

Below left: The 416 between Leatherhead and Esher was transferred to Mole Valley Transport Services, who operated it with a Ford Transit minibus. *John Glover*

Right: The 705 sees the use of an AEC Reliance, categorized by London Transport as RC. It is 1966 and RC8 is on the 705 to Sevenoaks, heading down Park Lane. *AEC/Ian Allan Library*

800	STEVENAGE, Bandley Hill, Longmeadow, STEVENAGE (Circular), then HITCHIN or MARTINS WOOD or SISHES END
800A	LONGMEADOW, Stevenage Industrial Area, HITCHIN. Certain journeys run between Stevenage Industrial Area and Stevenage Bus Station (Circular)
801	STEVENAGE, Long Meadow, Bandley Hill, STEVENAGE (Circular), then HITCHIN or MARTINS WOOD or SISHES END
801A	ITCHIN, Stevenage Industrial Area, LONGMEADOW. Certain buses run between Stevenage Industrial Area and Stevenage Bus Station (Circular)
803	Express. MAPLE CROSS, Rickmansworth, Croxley, Watford, Garston, St Stephens, St Albans, Smallford, New Hatfield, WELWYN GARDEN CITY STATION
804	HARLOW (Staple Tye), Harlow Bus Station, LATTON BUSH
804B	HARLOW (Kings Moor), Harlow Bus Station, LATTON BUSH
805	POTTER STREET, Brays Grove or Bush Fair, Harlow Bus Station, Harlow Town Station, LITTLE PARNDON
807	LETCHWORTH, Letchworth Gate, Weston, STEVENAGE
808	CHELLS, Bandley Hill, Longmeadow, Bedwell, Stevenage Bus Station, Little Wymondley, HITCHIN HOSPITALS (Limited Stop Service)
809	STEVENAGE STATION, Stevenage Bus Station, Bedwell, CHELLS

The Green Line routes are shown as they appeared in the London Country publication of June 1971.

701	GRAVESEND, Dartford, Welling, Blackheath, Victoria, Hammersmith, Brentford, Hounslow, Feltham, Staines, Virginia Water, ASCOT
702	VICTORIA, Hammersmith, Brentford, Hounslow, Feltham, Staines, Virginia Water, SUNNINGDALE (Mondays to Fridays peak hours only)
704	TUNBRIDGE WELLS, Halstead, Farnborough, Bromley, Victoria, Hammersmith, Osterley, Heathrow Airport, Slough, WINDSOR
705	SEVENOAKS, Sundridge, Westerham, Bromley, Victoria, Hammersmith, Osterley, Heathrow Airport, Slough, WINDSOR
706	AYLESBURY, Tring, Berkhamsted, Kings Langley, Watford, Edgware, Cricklewood, Marble Arch, Victoria, Brixton, Streatham, Croydon, Sanderstead, CHELSHAM. Extended from Chelsham to WESTERHAM during Monday to Friday peak hours, and from Westerham to CHARTWELL during the summer months
708	EAST GRINSTEAD, Lingfield, Godstone, Caterham, Purley, Croydon, Victoria, Cricklewood, Edgware, Watford, HEMEL HEMPSTEAD
709	GODSTONE, Caterham, Coulsdon, Purley, Croydon, Brixton, Oxford Circus, LONDON (BAKER STREET). This service is limited to a few journeys on Mondays to Fridays and on Sundays only

710	UXBRIDGE, Gerrards Cross, AMERSHAM	
711	REIGATE, Banstead, Sutton, Mitcham, Tooting, Oxford Circus, Shepherd's Bush, Ealing, Uxbridge, Gerrards Cross, Beaconsfield, HIGH WYCOMBE	
712	DORKING, Leatherhead, Epsom, Morden, Tooting, Victoria, Golders Green, Hendon, Radlett, Park Street, St Albans, Markyate, DUNSTABLE. (During the summer months, certain coaches run to WHIPSNADE PARK ZOO). Runs between St Albans and Dunstable during Monday to Friday peak hours and Sundays only	
713	DORKING, Leatherhead, Epsom, Morden, Tooting, Victoria, Golders Green, Hendon, Radlett, Shenley, St Albans, Markyate, Dunstable. (During the summer months, certain coaches run to WHIPSNADE PARK ZOO). Runs between St Albans and Dunstable during Monday to Friday peak hours and Sundays only	
714	DORKING, Leatherhead, Chessington, Kingston, Richmond, Hammersmith, Oxford Circus, King's Cross, Highgate, Barnet, St Albans, Harpenden, LUTON	
715	GUILDFORD, Esher, Malden, Barnes, Hammersmith, Oxford Circus, Wood Green, Enfield, Cheshunt, Hoddesdon, Ware, HERTFORD	
715A	GUILDFORD, Esher, Kingston, Barnes, Hammersmith, Oxford Circus, Wood Green, Enfield, Cheshunt, Hoddesdon, Ware, HERTFORD (Saturdays only)	
716	CHERTSEY, Addlestone, Weybridge, Hampton Court, Kingston, Richmond, Hammersmith, Baker Street, Finchley, Barnet, Hatfield, Welwyn Garden City, Welwyn, Stevenage, HITCHIN	

716A WOKING, Addlestone, Weybridge, Hampton Court, Kingston, Richmond, Hammersmith, Baker Street, Finchley, Barnet, Hatfield, Welwyn Garden City, Welwyn, Stevenage, HITCHIN

718 HARLOW, Potter Street, Epping, Loughton, Chingford, Tottenham, Finsbury Park, Oxford Circus, Victoria, Putney, Kingston, Staines, Egham, WINDSOR

719 HEMEL HEMPSTEAD, Leverstock Green, Watford, Stanmore, Neasden, Marble Arch, Victoria, Eltham, Swanley, Farningham, WROTHAM

720 BISHOP'S STORTFORD, Old Harlow, Harlow, Epping, Loughton, Woodford, Leytonstone, Stratford, LONDON (ALDGATE)

721 BRENTWOOD, Gidea Park, Romford, Chadwell Heath, Ilford, Forest Gate, Stratford, LONDON (ALDGATE)

723 TILBURY (Ferry), Chadwell St Mary, Grays, Rainham, Dagenham, Barking, Poplar, LONDON (ALDGATE)

723A GRAYS, Belhus, Rainham, Dagenham, Barking, Poplar, LONDON (ALDGATE)

724 Express. ROMFORD, Epping, Harlow, Ware, Hertford, Welwyn Garden City, Hatfield, St Albans, Watford, Amersham, HIGH WYCOMBE (Limited Stop Service)

725 GRAVESEND, Dartford, Sidcup, Bromley, Croydon, Sutton, Kingston, Ashford, Staines, WINDSOR

727 Express. LUTON AIRPORT, Luton, Harpenden, St Albans, Watford, Rickmansworth, Uxbridge, Heathrow Airport, Teddington, Kingston, Ewell, Epsom, Reigate, Gatwick Airport, CRAWLEY (Limited Stop Service)

Appendix B

The Garages

At 1 January 1970, London Country Bus Services inherited 28 garages. New garages were opened subsequently, at Crawley, Dartford and Slough. Outstations operated by LCBS are omitted. Unless otherwise stated, the garage was still in operation at the time of transfer to the private sector.

Code	Name	County	Notes
CM	Chelsham	Surrey	
CY	Crawley	West Sussex	New Crawley garage opened 1982
DG	Dunton Green	Kent	
DS	Dorking	Surrey	
DT	Dartford	Kent	New Dartford garage opened 1986, also incorporating Swanley
EG	East Grinstead	West Sussex	Closed 1981
GD	Godstone	Surrey	
GF	Guildford	Surrey	
GR	Garston	Hertfordshire	Renamed Watford 1979
GY	Grays	Essex	
HA	Harlow	Essex	
HE	High Wycombe	Buckinghamshire	Closed 1977
HF	Hatfield	Hertfordshire	
HG	Hertford	Hertfordshire	
HH	Hemel Hempstead	Hertfordshire	
LH	Leatherhead	Surrey	
LS	Luton	Bedfordshire	Closed 1977
MA	Amersham	Buckinghamshire	
NF	Northfleet	Kent	
RE	Romford	Greater London	Closed 1977
RG	Reigate	Surrey	
SA	St Albans	Hertfordshire	
SL	Slough	Berkshire	New Slough garage opened 1984, replacing Windsor
ST	Staines	Surrey	
SV	Stevenage	Hertfordshire	
SJ	Swanley	Kent	Closed 1986, see Dartford
TG	Tring	Hertfordshire	Closed 1977
WR	Windsor	Berkshire	Closed 1984, see Slough
WY	Addlestone	Surrey	

The County Council names are those during the period of LCBS's existence. Relatively few of the LT/LCBS garages are still in use today; just Dartford, Garston, Guildford, Harlow, Northfleet and Slough remained as at mid-2006, and different sites are used at Grays, Hemel Hempstead and Stevenage.

The sad remains of Reigate Bus Garage in September 2005, its doors very firmly closed for good as far as buses are concerned. *John Glover*

Appendix C

County Council Policies

The Transport Act 1985 (section 63(b)) required each County Council to make a formal statement of its policies regarding the provision of public passenger transport policies. This is the text of the second such document published by Surrey County Council, which came into force on 1 August 1989. The second rather than the first such document has been chosen, since three years after deregulation it includes changes made in the light of experience.

OBJECTIVES

The County Council have objectives of each of the various areas of public passenger transport:

Local Bus Service

To promote the provision of services which take account of the differing needs of communities in urban, suburban and rural areas, including persons who are elderly or disabled.

To promote the quality and reliability of all local bus services.

Secured Local Bus Services

To secure the provision of services which the County Council consider to be socially necessary in accordance with the provisions of existing transport legislation, and which match service levels with demand, but within the pre-determined budget guidelines.

Commercial Local Bus Services

To work with and, where applicable, to enter into agreements with, the operators of local public transport services and other bodies to promote positively the development of a public transport network which encourages patronage.

Traffic Congestion

To encourage the provision and usage of all types of public transport facilities wherever these can make a positive contribution to the relief of traffic congestion in the County.

Rail Services

To seek the retention of the rail network within the County at the levels of service which reflect the demands made upon it, and to encourage where possible road-rail interchange in accordance with the principles stated in the Structure Plan.

This document is concerned primarily with local bus services.

POLICIES

Provision of Socially Necessary Services

The need for socially necessary services may arise for three broad reasons:

Where no commercial services are provided in a geographical area or in a given time period, as a result of complete service withdrawals by operators as being no longer viable, it is the County Council's policy:

1   To set value for money criteria which take account of the cost of providing contract services and the likely passenger usage when deciding whether or not to provide a service;

2   That where such criteria are not met, to take into account in descending order of priority:
  • Service to communities which have a demonstrable need, but which would otherwise be isolated;
  • Services conveying adults to work or pupils to their nearest available school (where there is no statutory provision under the Education Act);
  • Services conveying people for shopping, personal business and medical trips;
  • Services provided for any other journey purpose.

3   To reassess existing contract services annually in accordance with the above criteria, whether the contract is due for renewal or not;

4   To provide temporary services under the emergency provision if it is necessary to maintain a service while a full assessment is made;

5   To prepare and publish value for money tabulations of all contract services annually.

Where commercial services are revised to offer curtailed levels of frequency, coverage or scope, it is the County Council's policy:

6   To secure socially necessary services only if the new timings do not provide adequate capacity for existing patronage, or do not in the view of the County Council provide adequate opportunities for work, school, shopping or recreational purposes.

Where new demands or perceived demands arise, it is the County Council's policy:

7   To evaluate services as above, but in view of the likely speculative nature of demand, to take account of this in the contract period offered.

Competition may arise for a service which is already provided under contract. It is the County Council's policy:

8   To maintain their contractual arrangements with their suppliers of contract bus services, unless their concomitant duty not to inhibit competition becomes overriding.

Budgetary Constraints

The County Council attach great importance to the provision of socially necessary services. It is the County Council's policy:

9   To provide the resources necessary to retain overall journey opportunities, subject to evidence of need and availability of finance.

Community Transport

Community transport in Surrey has two distinct elements:

Services provided for the general public, but where there are very low levels of demand and an element of voluntary help is likely to be present;

Services provided for a specific section of the public, notably the mobility handicapped, often with specialist vehicles.

Leyland Olympian LR13 as turned out by London Country South West in Surrey County Council's centenary year, 1989. It is outside County Hall in Kingston. The design was by Ray Stenning of Best Impressions. *John Glover*

It is the County Council's policy :

10   To encourage local organisations to devise community transport schemes to meet low levels of service demand;

11   To provide financial assistance for community transport projects for the general public in accordance with their criteria for socially necessary services;

12   To provide financial assistance for services designed especially for the mobility handicapped using criteria which reflect the special needs of such persons.

Fares and Concessionary Fares

The County Council have few powers in respect of fares generally, but intend to maintain their two concessionary schemes. It is the County Council's policy:

13   To set a maximum fares scale to ensure that fares on the services contracted by Surrey County Council are not unreasonable;

14   To continue the existing County-wide concessionary fares scheme for the elderly and disabled on registered local services (only);

15   To continue the existing County-wide concessionary fares scheme for children aged 5 and under 16 during the defined peak hours;

16   To require contract operation of weekday evening services to accept return and period tickets issued by the daytime operator as valid for travel, and to extend the principle elsewhere if suitable conditions exist.

Publicity

The publicity programme has been successful, and is to be developed further. It is the County Council's policy:

17 To provide general passenger information by publishing and distributing timetables for all local bus services within the County, updated as necessary;

18 To appoint an agent on contract to produce maps, timetables and other publicity relating to passenger transport services;

19 To provide specific passenger information on secured services at the principal bus stops used by these services and at rail stations as appropriate;

20 To publish a map of all services annually; and

21 To respond to the progress of information technology, especially in its application to disseminating information on bus services to the public.

Operators and the Passenger Environment

The County Council attach great importance to high standards of operational reliability of all services. It is the County Council's policy:

22 That operators be encouraged to make maximum use of existing premises;

23 To promote the Passenger Transport Liaison Group as a body consisting of County Council Officers and representatives of operators, with the remit of conducting negotiations in respect of fares and other policies which the Council may wish to pursue, reviewing the operation of existing policies and recommending changes, and discussing any other matters of common interest;

24 That statutorily entitled children will only be sent by commercial local bus services where a satisfactory standard of operation is provided;

25 To encourage the continuing use of existing bus stations within the County; to influence the selection of suitable sites for bus stops; and to encourage District and Parish Councils to continue the provision of bus shelters;

26 To acquire and maintain all bus stops served only by contracted services and to arrange the display of service publicity where appropriate;

27 To contribute towards capital expenditure by operators of public passenger transport services where considered appropriate by the County Council;

28 To discourage-on street parking of buses and particularly overnight parking.

Tendering and Contracts

The County Council wish to ensure that the services which it puts out to contract are provided as efficiently and effectively as possible. It is the County Council's policy:

29 To secure those services provided as a result of their policies 1 to 8 of this document by putting services out to tender in accordance with the provisions of the Transport Act 1985;

30 To have due regard for the needs of the elderly and disabled when assessing the suitability of vehicles used on services secured by the County Council;

31 To use the 'de minimis' arrangements for securing services wherever it is considered appropriate so to do;

32 To review the services offered by all contracts annually, to ensure that they are meeting the purposes for which they were provided, and to take action as necessary;

33 To monitor the operation of all contract services;

34 To adopt 'minimum subsidy' type contracts, but to adopt other forms of contract where appropriate;

35 To ensure that only operators with the necessary financial resources, maintenance facilities and operating licences are awarded contracts;

36   To make provision within the contract to levy such penalties as may be appropriate if the conditions of contract are not fulfilled.

Consultation and Liaison
The County Council wish to ensure that all bodies with an interest in passenger transport provision are provided with an opportunity to comment on their policies. It is the County Council's policy:

37   To publish, and update as required, their public transport policies;
38   To consult with District Councils, adjoining County Councils, rail and bus operators and London Regional Transport when reviewing existing policies and before deciding on and implementing new policies;
39   To extend their consultation duties to the London Regional Passengers' Committee (LRPC) and to other organisations such as the Surrey Voluntary Service Council and Parish Councils, and to invite accredited representative bodies to make known their views;
40   To develop close liaison with the Metropolitan Traffic Commissioner and the South East Area Traffic Commissioner.

August 1989

Nigel Gray, Traffic Planning Manager, (left) talks to John Talbot, Operating Manager, at the launch of the BTL-class Leyland Tiger/Berkhof coaches. *Stephen Morris*

Appendix D *London Country Bus Services, Operating Department, 1982*

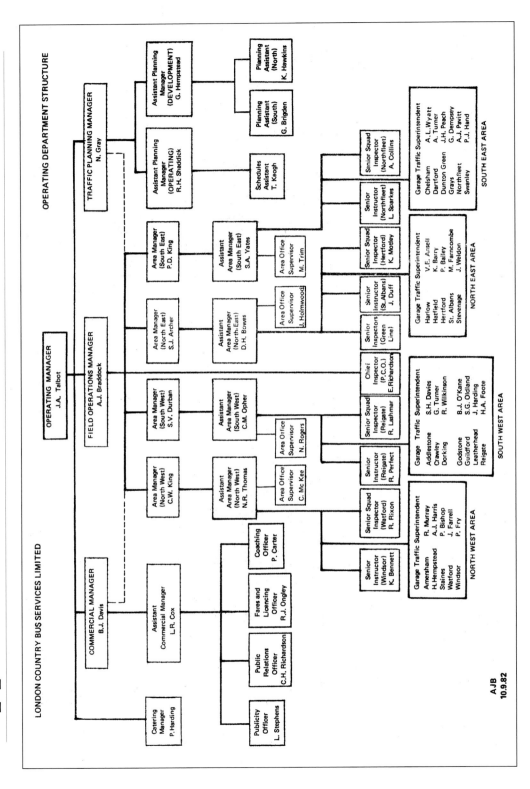

LONDON COUNTRY BUS SERVICES LIMITED

OPERATING DEPARTMENT STRUCTURE

AJB
10.9.82

Acknowledgements

My sincere thanks to the following who gave up their time and, in one way or another, helped me with material or their own reminiscences:

Don Benn, Guy Brigden, Tony Francis, Laurie James, Barry Le Jeune, Steven Salmon, Alan Teer, Geoffrey Wheatcroft, Keith White

I am also grateful to the Surrey Record Office for providing access to certain documents.

Bibliography

London Traffic Act 1924. HMSO

Road Traffic Act 1930. HMSO

London Passenger Transport Act 1933. HMSO

Transport Act 1947. HMSO

Rural Bus Services, Report of the Committee. Ministry of Transport, HMSO, 1961

Transport Act 1962. HMSO

Transport and Public Policy. K. M. Gwilliam. George Allen & Unwin, 1964

Public Transport and Traffic. Ministry of Transport, Cmnd 3481, HMSO, December 1967

Transport Act 1968. HMSO

Transport in London. Ministry of Transport, Cmnd 3686, HMSO, July 1968

The London Country Bus. J. S. Wagstaff. Locomotion Papers No 42, Oakwood Press, 1968

Transport (London) Act 1969. HMSO

London Transport Fares. Report No 159, National Board for Prices and Incomes, Cmnd 4540, HMSO, November 1970

Local Government Act 1972. HMSO

A History of London Transport, Vol 2 The Twentieth Century to 1970. T. C. Barker and Michael Robbins. ISBN 0 04 385063 4. George Allen & Unwin, 1974

Transport Act 1978. HMSO

Transport Act 1980. HMSO

House of Commons Transport Committee. Transport in London, HMSO 127-11, 1982

London Country Buses and Green Line Coaches. A background brief. LCBS undated, *c*1982

The Motor Bus in London Country. Kenneth Warren. ISBN 0 7110 1360 8. Ian Allan Ltd, 1984

Transport Act 1985. HMSO

National Bus Company 1968-1989 A Commemorative Volume. Compiled by John A. Birks with Yvonne Brittan, Keith A. S. Dickie and Tony Beetham. ISBN 0 86317 147 8. Transport Publishing Co, Glossop, 1990

National Audit Office Department of Transport. Report on the Sale of the National Bus Company, 1989

Annual Reports and Accounts of the London Passenger Transport Board, the British Transport Commission, the London Transport Executive, the London Transport Board, and the National Bus Company

Timetables of London Country, its predecessors and successors

Index

The 430 was for many years one of the most profitable of London Country's routes, providing the main town service in Reigate and Redhill. Dual-door AEC Merlin MBS271 is seen here on the A23 south of Redhill town centre in the early days of the company on 3 May 1970. Separate bus exit doors can be useful on busy urban routes, but can only be provided at the expense of seats. *John Glover*

By 1986, with deregulation looming, company timetables covering smaller areas were substituted for comprehensive books. All bore a common cover design as with this 'Travellers Times' for High Wycombe and Beaconsfield dated 4 January 1986. *Guy Brigden collection*

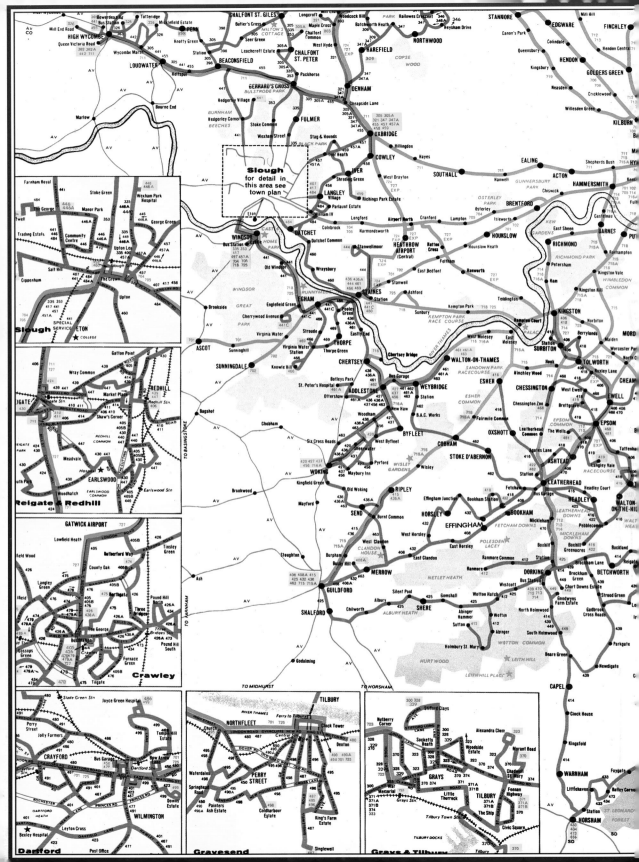